Praise for *The Portland Red Guide*:

A roller-coaster ride through Portland's radical past.
Who knew that being on the losing side of just about
everything could be so much fun?
    Phil Stanford, *Portland Tribune* columnist, author of
    Portland Confidential

Michael Munk is the Lewis and Clark of Portland's
radical past, leading his readers on a voyage of discovery
through a long-lost and wonderfully evocative historical
terrain. I only wish the *Red Guide* had been around in
the days when I was one of those Portland radicals he
writes about with such knowledge (and affection).
    Maurice Isserman, author of *If I Had a Hammer: the
    Death of the Old Left and the Birth of the New Left*,
    and former staffer at the *Willamette Bridge* and *The
    Portland Scribe*

Whoop! Whoop! I'm impressed by how many names
from Portland's past have not made it into our official
histories and public memorials. Some were good
friends of mine. Local history is too often overlooked.
Good work, Mike.
    Bud Clark, Saloon keeper, Goose Hollow Inn, and
    Mayor of Portland, 1985–1992

Michael Munk did a terrific job of researching
local leftist and labor struggles usually ignored by
conventional historians and the commercial media.
    Gene Klare, columnist, *Northwest Labor Press*. Former
    reporter, pre-strike *The Oregonian* and the *Portland
    Reporter*

What fun to learn all the ordinary places have a not-so-ordinary history.

Some will call *The Portland Red Guide* subversive, others will welcome it as the sweet breeze of revelation, but all will have to admit it adds a fascinating new layer to appreciating Portland.

Even those Portlanders who think they know their city's past will likely find themselves shocked at the wealth of radical Portland history related in this volume. One hopes it becomes as ubiquitous as cell phones in Portland pedestrians' hands.

Sandy Polishuk, author of *Sticking to the Union: An Oral History of the Life and Times of Julia Ruuttila*

Going to these addresses can bring to mind what has gone before and perhaps, encourage more resistance today. I had no idea so much has happened in Portland. And reading the names of people who struggled and whom I worked with brought up lots of memories.

Sandra Ford, former wife of Black Panther Party leader Kent Ford

The Portland Red Guide

Portlanders understand and appreciate
how differently beautiful is this part of the
world—the white city against the deep
evergreen of the hills, the snow mountains
to the east, the ever-changing river and
its boat life, the dusky oriental brilliancy
of Chinatown—and the grays, blues, and
greens, the smoke-dimmed sunsets and
pearly hazes of August. You don't have to
point out these things to our people.

—John Reed 1914

Let's drink a toast to all those farmers, workers, artists, and intellectuals of the last one hundred years who, without thought of fame and profit… worked tirelessly in their dream of a worldwide socialist revolution. Who believed and hoped a new world was dawning, and that their work would contribute to a society in which one class does not exploit another, where one ethnic group or one nation does not try to expand itself over another, and where men and women live as equals. The people who nourished these hopes and dreams were sometimes foolishly blind to the opportunism of their own leadership, and many were led into ideological absurdities, but the great majority of them selflessly worked for socialism with the best of hearts…The failure of socialism is the tragedy of the twentieth century and…we should honor the memory of those who struggled for the dream of what socialism might have been. And begin a new way again.

—Gary Snyder, May Day Toast,
for the Workers of the World, 2000

The Portland Red Guide

Sites & Stories of Our Radical Past

by Michael Munk

Ooligan Press 2007
Portland, Oregon

The Portland Red Guide
Sites & Stories of Our Radical Past

ISBN13: 978-1-932010-15-2

Cover design by Alan Dubinsky and Abbey Gaterud.
Cover image copyright Icky A.
Map design by T. H. McKoy V, Jason L. Schmidt, and David Banis.
Text set in Bembo Std and Helvetica Neue LT Std.

Library of Congress Cataloging-in-Publication information
available from publisher.

Ooligan Press
Portland State University
P.O. Box 751, Portland, OR 97207-0751
ooligan@pdx.edu   www.ooliganpress.pdx.edu
www.publishing.pdx.edu

10 9 8 7 6 5 4 3 2 1

Printed in the United States by United Graphics Incorporated.

To those who worked for a better world rather than their own place in the present one.

Table of Contents

The Portland Police Red Squad kept detailed surveillance records until the 1980s. Groups of all ideologies were monitored and photographed. This 1941 Communist meeting took place in downtown Portland. The numbers above the men's heads corresponded to their names, which were written on the back of the photograph. *City of Portland Archives, A2001-074.2.*

Preface

The Portland Red Guide developed from a childhood experience. As my school bus took me to the eighth grade in 1947, I was daily impressed by an imposing apartment building above the intersection of NW 23rd Avenue and Burnside Street. Perhaps that's why, after spending most of my working life on the East Coast, when I retired to Portland fifty years later and found the Envoy Apartments still standing, I decided to live there. A fellow tenant told me that John Reed, whom I admired as Portland's most famous Red, was born just above our building.[1] The steps at our back door that led up to SW Cactus Drive, he said, were all that remained of Reed's grandfather's mansion.

The City of Portland named the street next to us in honor of that grandfather—Henry Dodge Green—who one biographer says "got rich by swindling Indian tribes out of precious furs and using the profits to build water, gas, and iron empires,"[2] but Reed, the radical enemy of such exploitation, was ignored by his hometown. That made a perverse sort of sense to me: after all, don't those with the power to bestow municipal honors ensure they reflect dominant values rather than dissident ones?

Still, I considered the excitement stirred in me by sharing the physical space occupied by John Reed more than a century ago was similar to that evoked in visitors to more conventional historic sites. Could sites associated with such controversial Portlanders as Reed contribute to public interest in an alternative local history? Such musings inspired this *Portland Red Guide*.

I am grateful to that neighbor and the many friends, acquaintances, and informants who guided me to what is collected here. First were a quartet of visitors to my Gearhart beach shack—Steve Vause, Carlyn Synaven, the late Susan Wheeler, and Brooke Jacobson—to whom I evidently could not suppress my enthusiasm for exploring stories and sites of local radical history. Perhaps in an effort to quiet me down, they suggested, "Why don't you write it down?"

Among the many others whom I pestered for information are Elmer Buehler, Hank and the late Martina Curl, Eileen Cooke, Gene Klare, Bill Murlin, Norm Diamond, late members of the Old Men's Club Ken Fitzgerald, Nick Chaivoe, Jim Canon, and Ben Bartzoff, surviving members Charlie Grossman, Ed and Alice Beechert, Howard Glazer, and Virginia Malbin; and my colleagues at the Oregon Cultural Heritage Commission Tim Barnes, David Horowitz, Phil Wikelund, David Hedges, Walt Curtis, David Milholland, and the late Fred DeWolfe, who urged me to stay with the project when my energy faltered. Also, Ken Dragoon, Marvin Ricks, Harry Stein, Eugene Snyder, Lois and the late Jesse Stranahan, and many more whom I can only blame a diminished short-term memory for failing to acknowledge.

Ironically, one of the most rewarding sources for this guide was the archives of the Portland Police Bureau's infamous Red Squad, which contain records of its hostile spying on radicals, labor organizers, and civil rights and peace activists from the 1920s to the 1970s. It was Marcus Robbins, former city archivist, and assistant archivist Brian Johnson who introduced me to and guided me through that precious but outrageous material.

Extra credit should be granted to the skilled, dedicated, and enthusiastic students in Portland State University's Book Publishing program under Dennis Stovall's and his faculty's direction. While I spent the most time with Terra Chapek, Abbey Gaterud, Gloria Harrison, Vinnie Kinsella, and Carson Smith, I know that many others also edited, designed, and marketed the book in your hands.

Finally, special homage is due Kim MacColl, dean of local historians, whose monumental three-volume history of Portland pierced the fawning aura which conventional treatments had placed on its political and business leaders.[3] The late Gordon DeMarco, who distilled much of MacColl and added some original research,[4] was another valuable source. I should not forget Kim Fern's charming radical bike tour,[5] or Icky A's uniquely observed informal radical history.[6] Elsewhere, I was impressed by Bruce Kayton's *Radical Walking Tours of New York City* (2003), for which Pete Seeger wrote the introduction.

They all deserve whatever credit may come the *Red Guide's* way, but no responsibility whatsoever for my own errors, omissions, or poor judgments.

Michael Munk

Preface Notes

1. Gary Dennis, proprietor of a video store for film enthusiasts, had a similar epiphany when he read that his street, W. 103rd in Manhattan, was Humphrey Bogart's childhood home.

2. Tamara Hovey, *John Reed, Witness to Revolution* (New York: Crown Pub, 1975). Even the more polite biographers say Green's wealth was "derived from a particularly noxious form of commerce." Richard O'Connor and Dale L. Walker, *The Lost Revolutionary: A Biography of John Reed* (New York: Harcourt Brace, 1967).

3. E. Kimbark MacColl, *The Shaping of a City* (Portland, OR: Georgian Press, 1976); MacColl, *The Growth of a City* (Portland, OR: Georgian Press, 1979); MacColl and Harry H. Stein, *Merchants, Money, and Power* (Portland, OR: Georgian Press, 1988).

4. Gordon DeMarco, *A Short History of Portland* (San Francisco: Lexikos, 1990).

5. Kim Fern, "Portland Radical History Bike Tour" from Lewis and Clark College Political Economy Program (2002), http://www. lclark.edu/~polyecon/history%20tour.htm. See also Jason Wilson et al., "Jason's Portland Radical History-Tour" from Platial: the People's Atlas, http://www.platial.com/jason/map/5163.

6. "Livin' in Doom Town: History, Albina Gentrification, Dr. Marie Equi & Other Resistance," *Nosedive 8* 1997.

This rally, on August 1, 1932, was held outside the Japanese Consulate in downtown Portland. Protesters called for withdrawal from foreign wars, payment of the bonus, and other radical causes. *City of Portland Archives, A2001-074.92.*

How to Use
The Portland Red Guide

By linking our radical history to physical sites, I hope
to bring back to life and recognition the radical and
dissenting history of Portlanders—even if the physical
evidence of their life and times no longer exists. May
such modest sites evoke reflection on Portland's radicals
and the choices they offered. May they at least challenge
readers as Francis X. Clines did, in expressing hope for
a book on the consequences of a rumored slave revolt
in eighteenth century New York: such a book would
"burden any modern attempt at strolling the city's streets
in a spirit of innocence."[1]

It will soon become apparent to users of this guide that
the sites themselves will only rarely be physically impres-
sive and emotionally evocative. Architecturally significant
sites, such as the Pittock Mansion, are most often monuments to the privileges of the winners rather than the
ordinarily impoverished losers. So if we come upon, for
example, the unremarkable house on SW Hall Street
that was home to radicals Dr. Marie Equi and Elizabeth
Gurley Flynn, it's rather the link to their roles in local and
international radical history that might stir our curiosity,
not the structure itself. Similarly, the downtown site of the
Portland Police Bureau's Red Squad in the 1930s is listed
in the guide to reveal its infamous and continuing role
in suppression and harassment of local radicals. However,
there is nothing threatening or exceptional in what was
then the Railway Exchange Building and today is called
the Oregon Pioneer Building. As the director of the
Bosco-Milligan Foundation, Cathy Galbraith noted in its
register of Portland's black community's historic buildings,
"Sometimes a historic building doesn't look the way we
think a historic building should," but it should be respected because its "walls have witnessed history being made."[2]

Finally, even during the writing of the *Red Guide*, several sites yielded to the creed of "highest and best use" and were destroyed to enhance the profits of real estate speculators. Rather than eliminating the historic link entirely, the *Red Guide* notes at least some of those former sites. Readers seeking natural or man-made splendor, of which Portland boasts a fair share, are referred to page 244.

The guide groups sites in Portland and its vicinity into six broad historical periods which reflect how different radical and militant movements responded to the historical challenges of the day. Each period is introduced with a brief but pointed summary of its major trends and developments. The sites associated with each historical period are then generally arranged chronologically. The periods are:

A: The Nineteenth Century (Utopians & Marxists)

B: 1900–1930 (Wobblies & Socialists)

C: 1930s (Unions & Commies)

D: WWII–1960 (McCarthyism & Cold War)

E: 1960–1973 (Peaceniks & Civil Rights)

F: 1974–Present (Identities & Protests)

The significance of each listing in Portland's human history is briefly assessed and often illustrated. Each listing begins with a numbered star icon and the entry's title. Like this:

 Firebrand

Maps and illustrations are found at the end of each section. To find locations discussed in the text, look for the star icon on the maps. If an entry is illustrated, there will be a camera icon next to the title. Images are marked with their corresponding star icons. Throughout the book, if the subject of an entry is referred to elsewhere in the guide, the text is red with the appropriate section and listing number (e.g. Louise Bryant B19 in John Reed's listing). Within listings, titles are highlighted (e.g. **Ruth Barnett**), as are addresses (e.g. *4056 N. Williams Avenue*).

In each historical period, first mentions of organizations use the names in full with an abbreviation, but subsequent references within that period use just the abbreviations. For example, the first reference to the Industrial Workers of the World in section A is followed by the abbreviation (IWW), and subsequent references within that section are just the IWW. If a quick reference is needed, a list of frequently used acronyms is included on page 245.

The reader can use the guide in several ways. Reading the section introductions consecutively offers an informal narrative of Portland's radical history. Using the map and its location keys serves as a street or neighborhood guide to nearby sites. And for readers whose curiosity is aroused by a person, event, or organization on these pages—as is strongly hoped—consulting the endnotes, references, and suggested books and websites may be a first step toward becoming intimately familiar with their chosen subjects.

How to Use *The Portland Red Guide* Notes

1. "New York Burning: Gotham Witch Hunt," *New York Times,* October 2, 2005. In 1741, following false rumors of a slave revolt, thirty slaves and four whites were burned at the stake.

2. Darrell Millner, et al., *Cornerstones of the Community: Buildings of Portland's African American History* (Portland, OR: The Bosco-Milligan Foundation, 1995).

Radicals in Portland marched on August 1, 1932, in an antiwar rally at SW 4th Avenue and Main Street. As the marchers passed, a huge crowd looked on. *City of Portland Archives, A2001-074.90.*

Introduction

Class War and Revolution in Portland?

Portland's business and political leaders sure thought so. On the morning of June 8, 1934, the Board of Directors of the Portland Chamber of Commerce called an emergency session to hear a report from a select committee of several of their most prominent members. West Coast longshoremen had been on strike for a month, demanding union recognition and a shorter work week. The city's business leaders declared the strike a "siege on Portland industry."[1] Citing closed mills, rotting perishables on the docks, and industries shut down from lack of supplies, they denounced the city's police as insufficiently enthusiastic about protecting strikebreakers and the state's governor as unwilling to call out the National Guard. When they demanded decisive action to break the strike, the business leaders were warned by an army intelligence officer, "Portland is the worst hot spot in which to release troops at this time because if there is a revolution in the making, such action would precipitate it."

Although fully aware that "it would doubtless lead to bloodshed and perhaps loss of life," the Chamber charged its select committee to consider hiring armed vigilantes (deputized volunteers, it called them) to do the job.

The committee was chaired by Horace Mecklem, manager of the Oregon office of the New England Mutual Life Insurance Company, and included four other leading citizens: Henry Cabell of the Failing Estate, retired U.S. Army General Creed Hammond, attorney Ralph Hamilton, and lumberman Aubrey Watzek. Under the manifesto, "We must end this strike by peaceful means if possible, but if necessary, by other means," its members urged the Chamber to raise a private army to break the strike. The Chamber's members, in turn, with full appreciation that their vigilante army would probably cause bloodshed, signed on without recorded dissent. They set up a front organization called the Citizens Emergency Committee, which the Oregon Federation of Labor named the "silk stocking mob," and authorized it to hire between one thousand and five thousand vigilantes, whom the Chamber demanded Mayor Joseph Carson deputize as special police. With its private army of deputized police, the Chamber hoped to suppress Portland's "revolution in the making."

Governor Julius L. Meier (of the Meier & Frank department store) also saw the potential of revolutionary violence. Pleading with President Franklin Roosevelt to send federal troops, Meier declared, "We are now in a state of armed hostilities." He warned of an "insurrection, which, if not checked, could lead to civil war." After the President refused, Meier briefly mobilized Oregon National Guard troops at the Armory on NW 11th Avenue (now the home of Portland Center Stage's theater) before sending them to wait at a camp outside Portland.

The vigilantes hired by the "silk stocking mob" brought out the poets in striking longshoremen who published their efforts in *The Hook*, a mimeoed strike bulletin. One read:

> They must feel proud to be neatly clad
> In those "he-man" suits of olive drab;
> With a real live gun and a "billy" too,
> They plan great deeds, 'ere they are through.
> But our real men oft' have to smile,
> As they watch the specials all the while;
> Whole faces they have, though it won't be long
> 'Till they'll wonder just where their nose has gone.
> —P. F. Freeman

The mellow Portland of contemporary reputation and conventional history stands in sharp contrast to this remarkable episode from its past. Although conservative media such as *The Oregonian* may complain that the city's political culture consists only of the "kinda-liberal, liberal and commie pinko,"[2] most actual lefties would respond, "don't we wish." In any case, our opening story of Portland's brush with revolution more than seventy years ago indicates that its past includes some dramatic episodes largely ignored in our public history.

So the main purpose of the *Red Guide* is to offer a respectful rendering of the mostly-forgotten people, organizations, and events that challenged the dominant powers of their day in the name of justice and equality—of which the victory of the 1934 strikers is a remarkable exception to a long list of defeats. An informal guide to Portland's radical past, the *Red Guide* links notable radicals, their organizations, and their activities to physical sites associated with them. It honors those that the mainstream histories of Portland largely ignore.[3]

Who Gets to Name?

> Some of them have left behind a name, so that others can declare their praise. Of others, there is no memory; they have perished as though they had never existed. But these were also godly men, whose righteous deeds have not been forgotten.[4]

Like any other town, Portland sketches a public version of its history to residents and visitors through the names it chooses to bestow on city streets, buildings, parks, and natural features. The criteria for its more elevated celebrations (memorial plaques, commemorative monuments, published histories, and guides) are more selective. Few will be surprised that the honored names and sites are overwhelmingly those of Portland's land speculators and big businessmen, the winners in what has frequently been a corrupt struggle for profits from land and resource exploitation, and those fallen in American military missions—whether worthy or not.[5] As City Commissioner Sam Adams observed during the 2006 vote to rename North Portland Boulevard as Rosa Parks Way, "Most of Portland's streets are named for dead white developers or their daughters."

Alon Rabb added it up: "Portland streets bear the names of 100 businessmen, 92 landowners, 69 public officials, 46 real estate [speculators], 39 churchmen, 23 military men, and 7 lawyers."[6] Rabb then exercised his imagination to make his point:

> Riding my bike down John Reed Avenue, I turned towards tree-lined Louise Bryant Way and continued past Mark Rothko Plaza to War Resisters Square. It was a good feeling to move along paths bearing the names of two early twentieth century writers and revolutionaries and a painter with strong ties to our city, and wind up at a place commemorating peace. But the sharp horn of a restless driver awoke me from my reveries…I was hurled back to a city [whose names] hail not the people and deeds that contributed to my life, but captains of industry, politicians and corporations…As I ride along streets celebrating conquest and greed, I yearn for a time when such Portlanders as Linus Pauling and Don Chambers would be acknowledged. I keep hoping and pedaling.

Urban critic Lewis Mumford succinctly nailed the natural history of the American city from the beginning of the nineteenth century to the present day when he described it as "a private commercial venture to be carved up in any fashion that might increase the turnover and further the rise in land values."[7] At a 1938 address to the CITY CLUB OF PORTLAND F3, Mumford was impolite enough to denounce "certain persons" in his audience who were "licking their chops and counting their gold" from land speculation along the Columbia River and profit from Bonneville Dam.

If the official take on Portland's history celebrates only the values of a narrow part of the city's past, it can only tell a biased story. That bias not only relegates dissidents to "the dust bin of history," but also glosses over the corruption, stolen wealth, and crimes that enabled the winners. As the late Portland journalist Dean Collins asked, "Where do the leading businessmen, entrepreneurs, and real estate developers—many whose names appear on street signs and monuments—fit into the generation of dirty politics?" His answer was, "Everywhere…Portland only pretended it was different."[8]

The following *Oregonian* excerpt about the methods used to register "frequenters of dives" north of

W. Burnside illustrates the political corruption that plagued Portland's past.

> Some 10 days ago a well-known heeler went out on the streets and gathered in frequenters of dives, whom he led to the Eagle saloon, on First and Burnside streets, telling them that by coming there they would confer a favor on Police Sergeant Church. Once there, their names and ages were taken, and each was assigned a room in some North End lodging house. After the heeler had thrown a couple of $20 gold pieces on the bar and bought several rounds of drinks for all hands, they were loaded in three shipments on the First-Street car, taken thence to Washington, thence to Fifth and to the Courthouse, where they were duly registered by the heeler. That sort of thing has been going on in the North End for weeks, and such people may be depended upon to come out and vote the Simon ticket at the primaries tomorrow.
>
> Arrangements having been made for a full vote of the hobos and North End dive frequenters, it is urged that businessmen offset it by allowing their employees every opportunity to go to the polls tomorrow.
> —*The Oregonian*, February 23, 1902

> Tell me how you call a place, and I will tell who you are and what is important to you.
> —Alon Rabb, 1999

The significance of the power to name streets, cities, and even nations becomes clearest in the wake of revolution. When capitalism was restored in formerly socialist countries, nations such as the Soviet Union, Yugoslavia, and Czechoslovakia broke apart and were renamed. The pre-revolutionary names of St. Petersburg and Chemnitz replaced Leningrad and Karl-Marx-Stadt. But that political sea change could not dislodge the name of PAUL ROBESON D40, a frequent but controversial visitor to Portland, from the Berlin street named in his honor.

Portlanders witnessed the political significance of street names during World War I, when most streets with Germanic references were renamed, as if to clarify who our nation's enemy was. In the Brooklyn neighborhood, Frankfurt Street became our French ally Lafayette, and nearby Bismarck became Bush. Liebe Street, however, was spared because the City Council declared its pioneer namesake to have been a "loyal American."

Portland has some rules for naming its infrastructure, but in its rush to rename the most prominent portion of historic Front Avenue in honor of the late civic entrepreneur and World War II deportee Bill Naito, it violated a rule requiring the subject of a nomination to have been dead for five years. On the other hand, proposals to rename the Fremont Bridge over the Willamette River for the late Oregon Senator Wayne Morse have not succeeded, suggesting the outspoken opponent of the Vietnam War remains too controversial. What's wrong with Fremont? JULIA RUUTTILA'S F10 poem "The Fremont Bridge" explains:

> It dominates the skyline in Northwest,
> A high-arched span dwarfing the station clocks,
> Montgomery [Park], St. Helen's icy rocks.
> Named for a man who never knew or guessed
> The changes that time would bring to the west.
> Pathfinder, soldier, pioneer—
> Not with the plow—the extant and sword
> Were his true symbols, and that time is past…

There are important lessons to be learned from the lengthy struggle with racist undertones to rename Union Avenue (originally celebrating the North's victory in the Civil War) as Martin Luther King Jr. Boulevard. The original proposal to honor King by renaming downtown's Front Avenue for the civil rights martyr was blocked by the vigorous opposition of Portland's business leaders. The Portland City Council then voted to shift the name to Union Avenue in 1989, but a racist petition demanding the city council's decision be put to a public vote was circulated by the late fundamentalist Christian and former Republican state chair Walter Huss. Remarkably, fifty-one thousand Portlanders supported it. It was not until 1995 that the name was finally changed[10] when the Oregon Supreme Court ruled that naming streets was not subject to citizen initiatives because it was an administrative, not a legislative, act. Even then, persistent opponents, still led by Huss, tried but failed to change MLK Boulevard back to Union Avenue.

> Don't dig up the past! Dwell on the past and you'll lose an eye. Forget the past and you'll lose both eyes.
> —Old Russian proverb

A statue in King's honor was erected in front of the Oregon Convention Center at 777 NE MLK Boulevard several years later. More recently, the impact of the civil rights movement on racism permitted naming a school for the black freedom fighter Harriet Tubman; and in 2006 the new Rosa Parks School, named for the late anti-segregation heroine, was opened in the former World War II public housing complex, the rebuilt New Columbia Homes. The same year, proposals to rename Portland Boulevard "Rosa Parks Way" overcame opposition when the city council voted to make the change.

> It was Oregon, all right: the place where stories begin that end someplace else…There are worse things.
> —H.L. Davis, 1953

Today, names that evoke the original inhabitants of the land that became Portland survive mainly in the names of counties, while some references to Indian places by white settlers, such as the many Oregon creeks and other geographical features named for "Squaws," were decreed politically incorrect by the state legislature in 2001. In the early nineteenth century, the Portland/Vancouver basin was home to a resident population of four to five thousand Chinookian people that would swell to nearly ten thousand during the spring salmon run—one of the densest populations of American Indians north of Mexico.[11] Historically, the Chinookian tribe of the Multnomah lived along the Columbia from Sauvie Island to the Sandy River, while the Clackamas, Tualatin, and Clowewalla favored the area around the falls of the Willamette River at Oregon City. When President Thomas Jefferson sent his 1803 military expedition here "for the purposes of commerce," his Corps of Discovery passed Neerchokioo, a village where Portland International Airport now stands. The village contained twenty-five houses, fifty canoes, and two hundred residents called "Flatheads" by Lewis and Clark.

John McLoughlin, the British Hudson Bay Company's fur impresario, has a highway named for him between Portland and Oregon City. In contrast, the names of the five members of the Cayuse tribe who resisted Christian efforts to convert them—Telakite, Tomahas, Clokomas, Isiaasheluckas, and Kiamasumkin—are not found on Oregon City's Main Street. That's where Joe Meek, another celebrated pioneer hero for whom a Portland school is named, hanged them in sight of McLoughlin's mansion before more than one thousand spectators. Some historians and tribal members consider the 1850 execution that followed a trial run by Judge Orville "slippery as a greased eel" Pratt, "nothing more than a public lynching."[12]

From 1843, when the first provisional government formed a militia, until the United States invaded Cuba and the Philippines in 1898, Oregon soldiers fought only the native resistance—the Cayuse, Modoc, Nez Perce, and Bannock-Paiutes—killing almost two thousand of them while suffering less than one hundred dead. Even during the Civil War, most of Oregon's one thousand eight hundred Union soldiers did not engage the Confederacy but "pursued Native Americans around the Northwest."[13]

By the middle of the nineteenth century, Indian lands had been commercially or forcibly transformed through the Doctrine of Discovery[14] into a raw commercial venture called Portland (for its namesakes in Maine and England) and carved up among a handful of land speculators. The most prominent of these speculators were Asa Lovejoy, Francis Pettygrove, William Chapman, Daniel H. Lownsdale, and Stephen Coffin. They were soon followed by sea and riverboat captains Ankeny, Couch, Flanders, Hoyt, Irving, and Marshall. Among them, only Coffin's unfortunate name is absent today from any Portland street, school, or park.

By the end of the century, Portland had followed the natural pattern of urban development as power shifted from ownership of land to industry, utility franchises, railroads, banking, and trade. Winners in those enterprises—the Corbetts, Ladds, and Ainsworths, together with the MacLeays, Burnsides, Starks, and Bybees—joined the earlier speculators to become familiar names on the growing city's municipal landmarks. While wealth was a prerequisite to put a name on an official map, it was insufficient if not accumulated by Christian Anglo-Saxons. The official seal of the city includes the Star of David, but the city's wealthy Jewish families, the Hirsches, Franks, Goldsmiths, Sellings, and Meiers had to build or buy the property that carries their names.

Women, even those associated with powerful men and not known as dissenters, are almost absent from Portland place names. Local historian Eugene Snyder finds only North Ida Street and North Minerva Street in the St. Johns neighborhood, both the first names of wives of nineteenth-century land speculators.[15] Duniway School may have been named for Abigail the suffragette, but her given name isn't on it.

Finally, readers might be curious to know whom NE Marx Street commemorates, especially since the union halls of Bricklayers Local 500 and Cement Masons Local 1 are located at 12812 NE Marx Street. Given the bias in bestowing municipal names, it's safe to assume that it wasn't for Karl. On the other hand, between 1904 and 1907, Karl Marx was the name of a post office on the Oregon coast. Today, it's known as Neskowin. And, KARL MARX SALTVEIT C8 proudly identified an east Portland barbershop with his anglicized name (Carl Marx) in the 1930s.

Only a few of Portland's radicals, their organizations, or related events are officially acknowledged. The PGE Park Trimet stop offers a maintenance building decorated with writer Robert Sullivan's references to DR. MARIE EQUI B6, JOHN REED B20, *FIREBRAND* A5, and BEATRICE MORROW CANNADY B23, the first black woman to graduate from the Northwest College of Law in 1922, as well as a copy of a handbill defending labor leader Harry Bridges. Trimet's Portland Expo Center stop honors deported JAPANESE AMERICAN OREGONIANS D5 moved from the location's former livestock exposition center to concentration camps during World War II. There is a park bench and plaque erected by the private Oregon Cultural Heritage Commission honoring John Reed near his birthplace in Washington Park as well as a private memorial in Lovejoy Park to Benjamin Linder F12, murdered by President Reagan's Contras in Nicaragua. Perhaps most imposing is the remarkable and little known homage paid by the federal—not the city—government to Woody Guthrie D2, F23 at the Bonneville Power Administration's headquarters. Since 1990, Portland radicals, led by members of the band General Strike, have commemorated Joe Hill B9 on November 19, the date of the Wobbly songmaster's murder by the state of Utah. But the single exception to the city's (and Oregon's) reluctance to honor local labor leaders may be the floating dock on the Willamette River in downtown Portland that is named for longshore leader Francis Murnane F6.

Of course, there is no massive, popular demand in Portland that radicals or their works should be commemorated. Many Portlanders probably agree with the Kent, Ohio resident who dissented from a proposal for a memorial to the four students killed by National Guard troops while protesting during the Vietnam War, observing, "If for every death in a social movement anywhere in the U.S. we put up a memorial, we'd have them all over the place." But another Kent resident confirmed that ideology remains the dominant force in deciding who gets to be honored. Those who were killed in the 1970 "Kent State Massacre," he said, were only "some hippie college students who didn't know the meaning of law and order," and expressed a typically know-nothing view of history itself. "We should have stopped talking about them a long, long time ago."[16]

Final Thoughts

The endeavor
To interpret a city
Airily,
By a mere wave of one's words—
Presumptuous
A task for fools.
Come, fool!
—Mary Carolyn Davies, 1924

From the nineteenth century, when the earliest sites in this guide are dated, to the present day, many Portlanders have challenged the conventional wisdom that a capitalist economic system provides the best opportunities for personal and economic freedom and prosperity. As enshrined in stained glass over a hundred years ago in British Columbia's provincial capital building, the dominant credo has been: "The [capitalist] economy: without it, no wealth; with it, no poverty." But local radicals used to argue much more vigorously than today that prosperity for the few depended on the suffering of a large reserve labor force of poor, unorganized workers, and small family farmers. They exposed the hypocrisy of capitalists who argued that accepting the risks of a free market exempted them from any public oversight while, as owners of railroads and lumber and mining companies, they used their political muscle to exploit public land and its natural resources. The early populists and environmentalists, who argued that such public treasure should be reserved for the benefit of the people, lost a righteous, but hardly equal, struggle.

Those who believe that the public has access to a "free market of ideas" must confront the historic fact—for which this guide provides the example of Portland in 1934—that whenever those with vested private economic interests imagined any serious challenge to their dominance, they could count on obliging city and state authorities to suppress the threat. The most ferocious government persecutions of such radicals were conducted during the first Red Scare following World War I and the Russian Revolution, and again in the McCarthy Era following the Soviet-United States victory in World War II.

> Only a few of their names can be found in our school books. Fewer still stand in marble or bronze in our halls and parks. The mass of Americans knows little or nothing about them. Never mind. They dreamed nobly, and they acted.
> —Stewart Holbrook, 1957

It remains the dominant contemporary American ideology that something called human nature demonstrates that capitalism provides the most natural model for organizing our economic, social, political, and cultural affairs. Acting on the belief that all are born selfish and programmed to compete against everyone else may indeed help one survive in our present system and occasionally even succeed. But capitalism motivates people not only by offering the carrot of opportunity to an aspiring Nike entrepreneur, but also the stick of what awaits losers, publicly displayed on Skidroad—as Portland's lower West Burnside Street was known.

Most of the people, organizations, and events commemorated in this guide challenge that view of human nature. They testify, to the contrary, that many of them were motivated to improve the condition of the world rather than their personal status in it. Its historical listings call attention to those who insisted on a better justification for their lives than "success" in the struggle for material wealth, and so dedicated themselves to offering alternative visions of how to organize our economic and social affairs. That so far the majority of us have not been persuaded to sign on to their proposals, or that some of them gave up or even eventually succumbed to the dominant ideology, does not diminish the worth of their struggle.

Mike Davis succinctly expressed a bias, similar to that which readers will no doubt discover in this guide, when he stated, "the finest embodiments of moral courage in American history [were the] Abolitionists, the Wobblies B7, the Abraham Lincoln Brigade C27, and the Student Nonviolent Coordinating Committee."[17] But a listing in this book does not attest that a person has an unblemished political and personal history, nor that all the activities of every organization or every radical event were justified or successful. Adopting such standards would produce a small volume indeed, and if municipal officials used them, they would find it difficult to name any of our parks and streets. It should also become evident that not every one of our listees may have looked back on their radical activities with pride; indeed a few may have done so with great regret. No matter. The impulse they shared—the struggle for a better world rather than for their individual prospects in the existing one—is a righteous commitment that deserves wider and more generous public recognition.

Introduction Notes

1. Michael Munk, "Portland's 'Silk Stocking Mob:' The Citizens Emergency League in the 1934 Maritime Strike," *Pacific Northwest Quarterly*, Summer 2000:150–60. Reprinted in John Trombold and Peter Donahue (eds), *Reading Portland: The City in Prose* (Portland, OR: Historical Society Press, 2006). All quotes related to these 1934 events are from the files of the Portland Chamber of Commerce, held in the University of Oregon Library's special collections. They are fully documented in the above-noted article.

2. Ryan Frank, "A clear case of the blues," *The Oregonian*, July 6, 2006.

3. The distortion or selective ignoring of dissident history is not confined to Portland. See James W. Loewen, *Lies My Teacher Told Me: Everything Your American History Textbook Got Wrong* (New York: New Press, 1995).

4. This quote was used by the granddaughter of CIA director William Colby at his funeral. It begins by acknowledging rulers known for their valor and advisors for their intelligence but honors CIA agents killed in the line of duty for whom there is "no memory."

5. Dolores Hayden, *The Power of Place: Urban Landscapes as Public History* (Cambridge, MA: MIT Press, 1995) observes that the many equestrian statues of white males and cannons in the municipal parks of American cities are inspired by "John Wayne conquest stories." In 2006, critics opposed a Salem statue commemorating the U.S. soldiers who died in the Iraq invasion and occupation as premature and supportive of an unpopular war.

6. Alon Rabb, "Place names are about who has power," *The Portland Alliance*, May 1999.

7. Lewis Mumford, *The City in History* (New York: Harcourt, Brace & World, 1961) 426.

8. Quoted by John Terry, "Dirty Deeds Shaped Early Portland, too," *Oregon's Trails, The Oregonian*, November 20, 2005.

9. Julia Ruuttila, *This is My Shadow* (Self-published manuscript, 1989).

10. John Terry, "Ladd's House Stands its Ground," *Oregon's Trails, The Oregonian*, April 16, 2006. The U.S. Geological Survey, with advice from state authorities such as the Oregon Geographic Names Board decides the names of natural things: rivers, mountains, some historic sites. But roads, parks, etc. are "administrative designations...bestowed by the government under whose jurisdiction they fall—states, counties, cities, park districts, etc."

11. Robert T. Boyd and Yvonne P. Hayda, "Seasonal Population Movement along the Lower Columbia River: the Social and Ecological Context," *American Ethnologist* (1987) 309–25.

12. "Cold Trail of Pioneer Mystery Reaches Present," *The Oregonian*, September 29, 1996. Also see Ronald Lansing, *The Juggernaut: The Whitman Massacre Trial of 1850* (Pasadena, CA: Ninth Judicial Circuit Historical Society, 1993).

13. Francis Fuller Victor, *The Early Indian Wars of Oregon* (Salem, OR: F. C. Baker, state printer, 1894).

14. The Doctrine of Discovery legitimized "Christian" hegemony over Indian ("infidels, heathens, and savages") lands and was confirmed by the Supreme Court (*Johnson v. McIntosh*) in 1823. See also *Oregon's Future: a nonpartisan public affairs magazine*, Winter 2006, 68.

15. Eugene Snyder, *Portland Names and Neighborhoods* (Portland, OR: Binford and Mort Publishing, 1979).

16. *The Oregonian*, July 16, 1998.

17. Mike Davis, a former Reed student, is a "Marxist environmentalist" who teaches at the University of California, Irvine. Perhaps his best known work is *City of Quartz: Excavating the Future in Los Angeles* (London: Verso, 1990).

The Communist Party held this meeting in Lownsdale Square in 1941. *City of Portland Archives, A2001-074.7.*

This unidentified man used his donkey and cart to protest the actions of the powerful. His signs read "Free All Class Prisoners," "We're Against the Raw Deal & Stacked Deck," and "No Race Hatred." *City of Portland Archives, A2001-074.36.*

A: The Nineteenth Century
Utopians & Marxists

> Until the lions have their historians, tales of hunting will
> always glorify the hunter.
> —African proverb

The early history of dissenting Portland is largely the
story of people responding to the nation's uneven
economic past and expansionist adventures abroad.
The earliest listings include local manifestations of late
nineteenth-century populist agrarian, working class,
and anti-imperialist movements—a time that historian
E. Kimbark MacColl characterizes as one of "private
enterprise at the public trough." Against the devotion to
laissez faire capitalism that was the dominant ideology
of the time, some early organizations of wage workers were inspired by Karl Marx's systematic critique of
that economic system. The earliest such organization
was the Socialist Labor Party (SLP). Its Marxist ideology dates from 1890, but the party traces itself to the
Workingmen's Party in 1876. A Portland branch of the
SLP A1 continues to this day, educating its mainly elderly
members in a strict version of working class Marxism
that remains critical of rival socialist organizations. They
meet monthly at the Central Library.[1]

FIREBRAND A5, a national anarchist newspaper, was
published 1895–1897 from a farm in Sellwood until the
federal government suppressed it for obscenity. A sense
of how conservative Portlanders regarded anarchists
can be gleaned from a December 1901 article in *The
Oregonian:*

> An anarchist of the genuine stripe visited all that district
> south of Powell Street Saturday, peddling from house
> to house literature, whose teaching was the long line
> of anarchism. He carried with him several publications

which he offered for sale at all the houses visited. He timed his visits when he felt sure he would only find the women at home, about 4 o'clock in the afternoon. To those who declined to purchase papers of him, and very few did buy from him, he was very insulting. He said, among other things, that "Roosevelt would go the same way McKinley did, and it will not be long, It would serve him right, too."

Less exclusive and sectarian than the anarchists or the Marxist SLP was an agrarian and working class populist movement that blamed plutocratic monopolies and bankers for the recurring depressions that regularly cost millions of people their farms and jobs. The populists also opposed imperialistic adventures like the Spanish-American War, which, they charged, sent poor people to war to enhance the profits of the rich. Male Oregonians (women could not vote until 1913) expressed support for that movement through the Populist Party. In 1892, the Populist Party's presidential candidate, James Weaver, won 34 percent of the state's male population's ballots and sent several of its members to the state legislature. Four years later, 48 percent of Oregon voters backed William Jennings Bryan's coalition of the Populist Party, Democrats, and a splinter of Republicans. Bryan fell only two thousand votes behind the winner William McKinley, whose victory MacColl credits to "massive vote fraud."

In 1887, Oregon was the first state to formally declare the first Monday in September as Labor Day. Although it was later used to discourage American workers from observing the more radical international May Day, the Grand Marshal of New York's first Labor Day parade declared that the day was intended to "offer monopolists and their tools in both political parties such a sight as will make them think more profoundly." In recent years, Portlanders have observed both May Day and Labor Day.

Members of Portland's working class joined COXEY'S ARMY A4 in 1893 in its march on Washington to demand jobs for the unemployed.

Portland's municipal government and its business leaders celebrated what the radicals and populists opposed, and they heaped special honor on the first major military effort of U.S. imperialism. The Second Oregon Volunteer Infantry Regiment's (today's National Guard) participation in the 1898 invasion and occupation of the Philippines is celebrated in LOWNSDALE SQUARE A7. Together with today's Chapman Square, the adjoining squares are called the Plaza Blocks. In 1922, Portland also honored a hero of the 1898 U.S. invasion of Cuba—a greater success than its more recent effort at the Bay of Pigs—with A. Phimister Proctor's mounting of Rough Rider Teddy Roosevelt, on his horse, in the Park Blocks before the Portland Art Museum. Relics of the battleship *Oregon*, which participated both in the Philippine and Cuban invasions and the U.S. intervention against the Bolsheviks in the 1919 Russian Civil War, are proudly displayed at several locations in Waterfront Park and are also celebrated in a permanent exhibit at the Oregon Historical Society. In the 1930s, the late Oregon political leader MONROE SWEETLAND C25 called the *Oregon* a "propaganda battleship" that "glorifies the entirely uncalled-for war against Spain, which Americans should be eager to forget."

Another group of nineteenth-century dissenters chose to establish utopian communities instead of directly challenging industrial capitalism. Agricultural in nature, these communities were located outside the city and were based on common ownership and collective work. But some—none of which survived—were nearby, including the Aurora Colony (1878), SOCIALIST VALLEY (1895) A3, Nehalem Valley Cooperative Colony (1886), Bellamy (1897), and, far away in Douglas County, New Odessa (1882).[2] The Byrdcliffe Arts Colony that later became famous in Woodstock, New York, was originally planned by Ralph Radcliffe Whitehead and Hervey White near Alsea in 1901 but was soon abandoned.[3]

Although Oregon's black community numbered only 1,105 in 1900 (of whom about 70 percent resided in Multnomah County) and the state's constitution contained prohibition against black, Chinese, or "mulatto" residence, suffrage, and other civil rights, an AFRO-AMERICAN LEAGUE A8 was established in Portland by 1898. Many Portland-rooted black families can trace their histories to the Portland Hotel, which originally hired seventy-five black employees when it opened in 1880, and to the national railroads, which came shortly afterward and made the Pullman porter one of the more secure jobs open to black people.

Early Portland's race riots were white attacks on Chinese workers. The economic depression of 1884 persuaded some jobless workers and even union organizers that, rather than capitalism, their plight was caused by Chinese workers, originally recruited to build the western railroads. In 1886, white mobs kidnapped one hundred and sixty Chinese workers at the Oregon City Woolen Mills and marched them to the Plaza Blocks. There, a torch-carrying mob of over one thousand white people demanded they leave town.[4]

 Socialist Labor Party Meetings

The handful of surviving members of Local Section Portland of the historic **SLP** still meet monthly in the Multnomah County Central Library at *801 SW 10th Avenue*. Outside Portland, Astoria's former SLP hall exists as a mid-century time capsule in the Bergerson Tile and Stone store at 1796 Exchange Street.[5]

 Mary Leonard

The first woman to practice law in Oregon, **Mary Leonard**, finally succeeded in 1886 after a long and hard-fought battle in the State Legislature and Supreme Court. Her legal career was stimulated by the months she spent in the Wasco County jail before being acquitted of murdering her ex-husband. But her career ended in 1912 when she walked out of court in Portland. She was found ill and alone a few months later in a little house on E. Washington Street and died in the Multnomah County poor farm (now McMenamin's Edgefield Manor, 2126 SW Halsey Street in Troutdale). Her body was donated to the University of Oregon Medical School, today's Oregon Health Sciences University.

3 Socialist Valley Road

Arguably America's only public road commemorating
socialism is in Polk County near Portland. Socialist Valley Road led from Fall City to Socialist Valley, founded
in 1895 as one of the cooperative settlements that
flourished briefly in the state. The town sent $10 to the
Socialist Party as its monthly dues in May 1907, but by
1920 the town was abandoned and nature was retaking
its site. The Oregon Department of Transportation also
lists the Socialist Valley Bridge, on Socialist Valley Road
over the Little Luckiamute River.

4 The Fifth Regiment of Coxey's Army

The Fifth Regiment of Coxey's Army was recruited
by local organizer Jack Short at **SW 3rd Avenue and
Burnside Street** in 1894, with the support of the Central Labor Council and a contingent of fifty brought up
from San Francisco by Captain Kain—whose "advance
party" of four included three black members. A major
economic depression had inspired an Ohio businessman, Jacob Coxey, to organize a march on Washington
by what he called a "United States Industrial Army" to
demand hundreds of thousands of road-building jobs
for the unemployed. While in Portland, Coxey supporters engaged in furious debate with both *The Oregonian*,
which called them "a mobilization of bandits [and]
a menace to law and order," as well as with the City
Board of Charities which regarded them as "organized
vagrants for the purpose of terrorizing the community."
Kain fired back: "We are starving in a land of plenty.
Why?" At one of their rallies held at their camp near the
Southern Pacific rail yards, one thousand five hundred
Portlanders came out to lend their support.

Intending to take over a train bound for Washington,
D.C., the 446 men of the Fifth Regiment now led by
stonemason E. F. Schier occupied an eastbound train
at the Troutdale depot on April 28, 1894. They were
arrested by federal troops one hundred and twenty miles
east of Portland, at Arlington, and returned to Portland

in box cars under heavy guard.[6] A trial, accompanied
by downtown rallies with over one thousand supporters, led to their apologies for breaking the law, and their
release. Most of them apparently left in groups of ten to
twenty-five on eastbound freights.

5 *Firebrand*

In 1895, the national anarchist weekly **Firebrand** was
launched from a farm in Portland's Sellwood neighborhood by Henry Addis, farmer and former SLP member,
Abner J. Pope, scion of a prominent New England
Quaker family, and Russian immigrant Abraham Isaak—
supported by Mary Isaak's laundry work. *Firebrand* first
appeared in January with the goal of filling in a perceived
gap in Portland's local papers. Addis explained:

> A little over a year ago comrade [J. H.] Morris was
> running a small job printing office in this city. Comrades
> Mary Squire [corset maker], A. Isaak, Ezekiel Slabs
> [gardener], John Pawson [woodcutter] and myself visited
> the meetings in the city where free discussion was had,
> and occasionally took part in the discussions. We also
> tried to get our ideas into the local "reform" press. We
> finally found all the columns of the press closed against
> us, except on condition that we "trim" our contributions.
> We talked the matter over and concluded to start a
> paper.[7]

The early issues of the paper reflect this localized
radical or reform community, including announcements
for Portland's Secular Union, events at the German
Turn Verein Hall F17, Knights of Labor union meetings,
Spiritualists, and the Central Labor Union. But the
paper quickly adopted a more militant anarchist outlook
and established itself as not just for Portland, or even the
West, but also for the whole Anarchist Movement.

Publication ended in 1897 when the three men were
arrested and convicted on federal charges of sending
obscene literature (a Walt Whitman poem) through the
mail. After their release from prison, Mary Isaak later
traveled with the anarchist leader and *Firebrand* contributor

EMMA GOLDMAN B22. Addis had arranged for one of Goldman's earliest visits to Portland in 1898, and in 1899 after her Portland lecture, Goldman visited Scio (founded by Czechs), where she met Gertie Vose, Donald Vose's mother, and the town marshal offered her use of city hall.

Herman Eich, a German Jewish immigrant called Portland's "rag-picker poet," wrote many of the poems that appeared on the front page of every issue of the paper, including "The Red Flag," which appeared in the second issue, and "Freedom," which appeared on September 6, 1896, together with his obituary, "Another Victim," by J. H. Morris. Eich, about 32, was killed riding the rods to promote the *Firebrand* in the east when a Union Pacific brakeman ordered him off a moving freight car in Rock Springs, Wyoming. He fell and was crushed under the wheels.[8]

 The Equal Suffrage Association

The Equal Suffrage Association, organized in 1896, had its first office at **294 SW Clay Street**. Speakers that year included county Judge J. A. Ward, who was welcomed as "another one of the manly men who are in perfect accord with their wives and daughters as advocates of equal rights for all people," and the learned Dr. Jinda Ram who spoke on the Hindu philosophy "from conception to cremation." Later, before World War I, the Equal Suffrage office was located in the Selling Building (today's Oregon National Building) at **610 SW Alder Street.**

 Lownsdale Square

Despite opposition from the local Anti-Imperialist League, the 1898 U.S. invasion and occupation of The Philippines and Cuba are celebrated by several monuments in the heart of downtown Portland. The oldest is in **Lownsdale Square** between the Multnomah County Courthouse and the Mark O. Hatfield U.S. Courthouse; it honors the Second Oregon Volunteer Infantry Regiment's participation in the war against Filipino independence. Ironically, this monument soon became the favorite gathering place for the early Wobblies and in the 1930s for the Communists' May Day demonstrations.[9]

During the war for the Philippines, CHARLES ERSKINE SCOTT (C. E. S.) WOOD B29 expressed his solidarity with the Filipino Resistance in a prominent western magazine published in Portland. "Were I a Filipino [and found that the United States] came with hammer and sword, not to strike off my shackles, but to rivet them faster," he wrote, "I would fight, fight, fight till the sun was blotted from my eyes."[10]

 8 Afro-American League

In a hall at **SW 2nd Avenue and Yamhill Street** in November 1898, Portland's **Afro-American League** held a mass meeting to protest a white terrorist attack on the elected city government of Wilmington, North Carolina, whose officials were mostly black. J. N. Fullilove (a barber who lived at 1732 SE Morrison Street), Rev. Shepard S. Freeman of the Bethel African Methodist Episcopal Church (then at **226 NW 10th Avenue**; Freeman lived at **314 Everett Street**), and E. McGee spoke. A petition to President McKinley was adopted proclaiming that "The colored citizens of Portland, Oregon…protest against the massacre and unlawful treatment accorded Afro-Americans in the city of Wilmington, N. C. and as many more in Greenwood, S. C."[11] In 2006, an 1898 Wilmington Race Riot Commission issued a report noting the racist attack in Wilmington in which an unknown number of black people were killed and many others forced to flee as the "only successful overthrow of a municipal government in American history," and laid the foundation for voter disenfranchisement in North Carolina.[12] In March 1900, "in a new departure for Oregon politics, thirty-four young men" signed up with the Negro Democratic Club at 82 NE 2nd Street and elected C. A. Hughes president, Grant Cross vice president, G. W. Hamilton secretary, and Pendleton Smith treasurer. It was later known as the Iroquois Club.

1. For meeting details visit the Portland SLP website at http://slp.pdx. home.mindspring.com.

2. James J. Kopp, "Documenting Utopia in Oregon," *Oregon Historical Quarterly*, Summer 2004.

3. "After a scandalous affair with a Miss Hart in California, Whitehead in 1901 enlisted the help of the writer Hervey White to help him plan another ideal commune. They chose a site near Albany, Oregon, in a spot so remote that self-sufficiency was the only way to stay alive. A group of musicians was dispatched in the fall to build the colony, by the time White and Whitehead arrived the following July, the settlers were all quarreling and the commune was abandoned before it began." Robert Edwards, "The Utopias of Ralph Radcliffe Whitehead," *Antiques* 1985.

4. In the 1970s, the Portland Labor Players produced a re-enactment of the story called *Season of Silence: Life and Labor in the Oregon City Woolen Mills*.

5. Astoria is also the birthplace of the famous radical photographer Consuelo Kanaga (1894–1978). She was the daughter of Clatsop County District Attorney Amos Kanaga and writer Mathilde Hartwig Kanaga. The family left Oregon for San Francisco around 1900, where Consuelo later began a career that took her around the world to document the class struggle. *She is a Tree of Life to Them* in the celebrated *1955 Family of Man* exhibition is one of the best-known photographs by a native Oregonian.

6. Dmitri Palmateer, "Charity and the 'Tramp': Itinerancy, Unemployment, and Municipal Government from Coxey to the Unemployed League," *Oregon Historical Quarterly*, Summer 2006.

7. Carlos Schwantes, "Free Love and Free Speech on the Pacific Northwest Frontier: Proper Victorians vs. Portland's 'Filthy' *Firebrand*," *Oregon Historical Quarterly*, Fall 1981.

8. For more on Eich, see Paul Avrich's *Anarchist Portraits* (Princeton: Princeton University Press, 1990).

9. Sean McEnroe, "Painting the Philippines with an American Brush: Visions of Race and National Mission among the Oregon Volunteers in the Philippine Wars of 1898 and 1899," *Oregon Historical Quarterly*, Spring 2003.

10. Charles Erskine Scott (C. E. S.) Wood, "Imperialism and Democracy," *Pacific Monthly*, June 1899.

11. *The Oregonian*, November 18, 1898.

12. *The New York Times,* June 3, 2006.

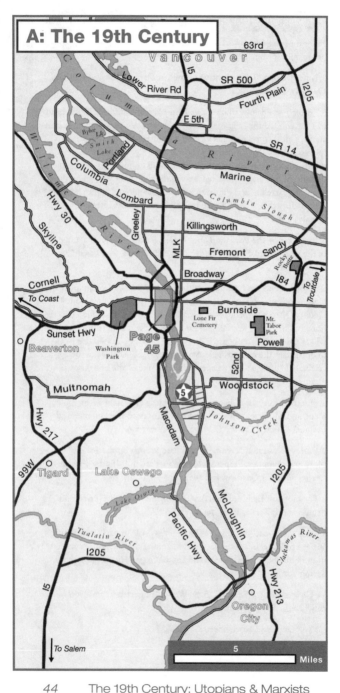

A: The 19th Century

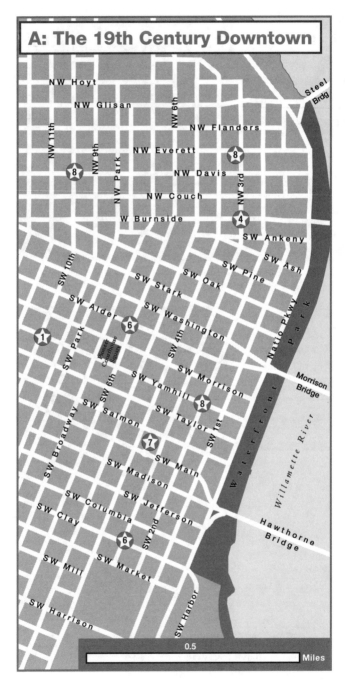

A: The 19th Century Downtown

NW Hoyt

NW Glisan

NW 6th

NW Flanders

NW 11th

NW 9th

NW Everett

(8)

NW Park

NW Davis

NW 3rd

NW Couch

W Burnside

(8)

(4)

SW Ankeny

SW Ash

SW Pine

SW Oak

SW 10th

SW Stark

SW Alder

SW Washington

(6)

SW Park

(1)

Pioneer Courthouse Square

SW 4th

SW Morrison

SW Yamhill

SW 6th

SW Broadway

SW Salmon

(8)

SW Taylor

SW 1st

(7)

SW Main

SW Madison

SW Jefferson

SW Columbia

SW 2nd

SW Clay

(6)

SW Mill

SW Market

SW Harrison

SW Harbor

Steel Brdg

Natio Pkwy

Waterfront Park

Morrison Bridge

Willamette River

Hawthorne Bridge

0.5

Miles

 Members of the Socialist Labor Party still meet monthly at the Multnomah County Library at 801 SW 10th Avenue. *Colin Smith*.

 Socialist Valley Road in Polk County. The road led from the town of Fall City to Socialist Valley, a cooperative settlement founded in 1895. It is, arguably, America's only public road commemorating socialism. *Michael Munk*.

THE FIREBRAND

For the Burning Away of the Cobwebs of Ignorance and Superstition.

VOL. I. PORTLAND, OREGON, SUNDAY, AUGUST 11, 1895. NO. 27.

| THE FIREBRAND | A SYMPOSIUM | thing left to do—take possession! Thi smeans |
| | ON | a revolution, which in all probability will in— |

Publication of *Firebrand*, a national anarchist weekly, was launched in 1895 from the Sellwood neighborhood by Henry Addis, Abner J. Pope, and Abraham Isaak. Publication ceased in 1897 when the three men were arrested and convicted of sending obscene literature through the mail. *Oregon Historical Society, microfilm.*

Lownsdale Square, between today's Multnomah County Courthouse and the Mark O. Hatfield U.S. Courthouse, was the favorite gathering place for Portland's radicals. This photo, taken at a Communist Party gathering, shows the monument to the Second Oregon Volunteer Infantry's involvement in the U.S. occupation of The Philippines and Guam in 1898. *City of Portland Archives, A2001-074.4.*

William U'Ren defended members of the Portland Communist Labor Party against charges of violating the state Criminal Syndicalism Act on March 10, 1920. U'Ren, middle-right, was flanked by the defendants, (from left) Claud Hurst, Fred W. Fry, and Karl W. Oster. Hurst was sentenced to two years in prison, Fry was given parole (he was deaf), and Oster was sentenced to five years in prison. *Oregon Historical Society, CN009663.*

B: 1900–1930
Wobblies & Socialists

During the first three decades of the twentieth century, the radicals of the previous century were followed by mass movements that more specifically offered the alternatives of Socialism and, after the Russian Revolution, Communism. The largest of these was the Socialist Party led by Eugene Debs. The Socialist Party was committed to electoral participation by urban workers and was most successful in rural areas. In 1900, Oregon's Socialist Party polled only one thousand five hundred votes, while William Jennings Bryan's Democratic Peoples' Party had a total of thirty-three thousand. But when Debs brought his campaign to Oregon in 1908, he drew large crowds and inspired radicals like Eugene's Floyd Ramp (1874–1973) to a lifetime of revolutionary commitment.

> Ten thousand persons at the Exposition Building last night heard Eugene V. Debs, Socialist nominee for President, excoriate the Republicans and Democrats as the instrument of the capitalist class. The demonstration that attended Mr. Deb's appearance in the Exposition building was remarkable. The instant the Socialist leader entered the hall, the signal was given and the band started up a lively air. Simultaneously the entire audience arose as one man and with shouts that shook the rafters of the building greeted their chief.
> —*The Oregonian*, September 15, 1908

Debs came to Portland on his campaign train, "The Red Special" with the "Red Special Band." The three-story Exposition Building stood on the north side of what is today PGE Park.

More than 10 percent of Oregon's voters (thirteen thousand) supported Debs for President on the Socialist Party ticket in 1912, with his strongest support not in Portland but in rural Josephine, Jackson, and Coos counties where he came in second. That high-water mark for the Socialist Party was also the year when a Socialist from St. Johns was elected city alderman in Portland, and socialists were elected as the mayor of Coquille and a councilman in Medford.

The number of Portland Socialist Party locals rose from five in 1907, when they joined the INDUSTRIAL WORKERS OF THE WORLD (IWW) B7 march to celebrate the acquittal of Wobbly leader William "Big Bill" Haywood, to nine in 1919. Six of those locals were foreign-language based. A Multnomah County Local of the Socialist Party still meets at the Belmont Library, 1038 SE 39th Avenue.[1]

The IWW, whose members were called Wobblies, was another radical working-class organization. However, unlike the Socialist Party, the IWW expressed contempt for electoral politics. Instead, it was committed to replacing capitalism by organizing the working class into one big union that, when strong enough, would refuse to work for capitalists and bring down the system. In 1907, in one of their first strikes anywhere, local Wobblies organized three thousand sawmill workers to walk out of Portland's saw mills and demand higher wages and shorter hours. Another Wobbly-supported strike against the OREGON PACKING COMPANY B13 in 1913 inspired some Portlanders to become prominent radicals, including DR. MARIE EQUI B6 and TOM BURNS C19.

The Oregon system of electoral initiative, referendum, and recall is an enduring child of the populist movement. In 1902, Oregon voters passed William U'Ren's direct legislation package based on support from the rural Grange and the labor movement. His People's Power League (1905) continued the struggle for clean government as they charged Portland's business leaders with widespread vice and corruption. A mayoral commission in 1912 listed 431 properties as "wholly given up to immorality." Their owners were well-known local "community leaders," including members of the Failing, Corbett, Reed, Weinhard, Ainsworth, and Glisan families.[2]

Limits on dissent were systematically imposed on opponents of the United States entry into World War I and continued after the war with the federal government's notorious Palmer Raids, jailing and deporting many radicals. In support of the Red Scare, the Oregon legislature passed the Criminal Syndicalism Act. The Portland Police Bureau established its infamous RED SQUAD F26, developed from a "reserve squad" originally created in 1914 to enforce Portland's vagrancy and vice statutes. By World War I, however, its scope had been expanded to include antiradical activities.[3] The ban on "vagrants" (defined as anyone having less than five dollars or so in their pockets) reflected the fact that great numbers of single men moved throughout the country during that era looking for work. In one of their songs, already well known by 1910, an Irish worker reflects unfavorably on his experiences in our "Portland County Jail."

> I'm a stranger in your city,
> My name is Paddy Flynn;
> I got drunk the other evening,
> And the coppers run me in.
>
> I had no money to pay my fine,
> No friends to go my bail;
> So I got soakt for 90 days
> In the Portland County Jail.

All three levels of government soon organized raids, mass arrests, vigilante assaults, and deportations of radical Portland groups, including Wobblies, Socialists, labor organizers, and antiwar agitators. U'Ren himself defended some of those arrested.

At the same time, the Russian Revolution (chronicled by Portland's best-known radical JOHN REED B20 in his *Ten Days That Shook the World*) set off a fresh surge of radical activity, including the organization of a Portland Soviet modeled after the Russian Soviets, and several varieties of a Communist Party.

The last major electoral effort of the populists came in 1924 when Robert M. LaFollette Jr.'s Progressive Party, a coalition similar to the earlier populists, came in second in Oregon with 25 percent of the vote—which now included women—and captured almost a third of the votes in the Portland area.

⭐ 1 William Z. Foster 📷

Former W. Burnside Street saloons are the sites associated with **William Z. Foster** (1881–1961), labor leader and longtime head of the U.S. Communist Party. He made Portland his home beginning in 1901, hoboing here until 1907. He worked in lumber camps, laid railroad track along the Columbia River near White Salmon, and shoveled heavy green railroad ties on the Portland docks, where he joined the Longshoremen's Union. Soon after his arrival, he shipped out for several years and returned to Portland in 1904 (just in time, he said, to join 7,618 other male Oregonians to vote for Socialist Party presidential candidate Eugene Debs). With his brother-in-law George McVey, he claimed three hundred and twenty acres (and a timber claim the same size) in the Mosier homesteads, calling it "a wild country, heavily timbered and full of fish and game, back of the famous Hood River apple district...south of the Great Columbia River...in the background loomed magnificent Mount Hood." After three summers, he gave up the land and ended what he called "the first and last time in my life that I ever attempted to gather together property."[4] After voting for Debs, Foster formalized his ties to radical politics by joining a Portland local of the Socialist Party, reading Marxist classics, and selling socialist newspapers in the streets. The Socialist Party's leader in Portland was Tom Sladen, whom Foster described as "a champion of working class culture who considered cuspidors 'bourgeois' and removed them from the party office." Foster also recalls the government kidnapping of IWW leader "Big Bill" Haywood and was probably among the three thousand workers who marched to protest in the IWW's first Portland demonstration on February 24, 1907. Five Socialist Party Locals joined forty of the sixty labor unions in the city that day.

During his Portland years, Foster frequented Skidroad bars, including Erickson's Saloon (recently the Barracuda nightclub) at **9 NW 2nd Avenue**. A sign above its entrance read, "A Workingmen's Club Known as Erickson's" well into the 1960s, but Foster's favorite hangout was across the street at the former Brazier Brothers Saloon, now **222 W. Burnside Street**. He recounts that the Brazier was so well known that on a railroad water tank at The Dalles, "I once read the following realistic poetic outburst of an eastbound hobo returning from the Pacific Coast."[5]

> I came out West for change and rest;
> But the whores got my change,
> And Brazier got the rest.

 Anniversary of the Emancipation Proclamation

THE AFRO-AMERICAN LEAGUE A8 held its annual celebration of the anniversary of the Emancipation Proclamation on New Year's Day 1902, at the AME Zion Church, **1229 SW Main Street**. This celebration "consisted of several musical numbers and addresses."

 1905 Lewis and Clark Exhibition Protest

Construction of Portland's Lewis and Clark Centennial and American Pacific Exposition and Oriental Fair in March of 1905 began with a picket line at its gates at **NW 25th Avenue and Vaughn Street**—an episode rarely noted in the celebratory histories of the event. At the time, *The Oregonian* found twenty-five pickets "chosen at a large meeting of workmen, following upon an unsuccessful attempt of agitators to call a general strike." Their demands were "not to be compelled to work with any but union men, recognition of their unions and an eight hour day." While the account hopefully predicted that "the pickets are not likely to be successful," it understood "the fact that all men hate to be called scabs" as "the only strong weapon in the hands of the pickets."[6]

 Harry Lane

A son of one of Oregon's prominent pioneers, **Harry Lane, MD**, was elected mayor of Portland in 1905 with working-class support and opposition from the business elite. He energetically exposed the long-standing practice of granting municipal franchises to political contributors. A city that "voluntarily consents to being assessed and taxed by a private corporation," he declared, "is unfit to exist." But Lane's vetoes of the city council's giveaways were usually overridden and, like many reformers, he failed to end municipal corruption. Elected to the U.S. Senate in 1912, his anti-imperialist stance led him to become one of only six senators to oppose United States entry into World War I, an opinion for which his enemies savagely attacked him. He died a month after that vote. His daughter Nina was a Socialist and married her comrade Issac McBridge, who became Lane's secretary in the Senate. Lane is buried in **Lone Fir Cemetery on SE 23rd Avenue and Stark Street**, where, in 1940, the Portland Peace Day Conference held a service in his memory.

 5 White Eagle Saloon

Today's popular music venue, the **White Eagle Saloon** at **836 N. Russell Street**, was named for the Polish national symbol when it opened in 1906 and a radical Polish group, Progress, was meeting in rooms upstairs. Reactionary local Poles falsely accused Progress of being anarchists plotting to assassinate President William Howard Taft.[7] That was enough for the Portland police and the Secret Service to raid the saloon shortly after it opened.

 6 Dr. Marie D. Equi

One of the first women to graduate from the University of Oregon Medical School (1903), **Dr. Marie D. Equi** (1872–1952), also was a militant fighter for workers' and women's rights. After setting up her medical practice, which included abortion services to both working-class and high-society women, she lived with her assistant, Harriet Speckert, in what is today's Mark Spencer Hotel (then the Nortonia Hotel) at **409 SW 11th Avenue**. Radicalized by police suppression of OREGON PACKING COMPANY WOMEN STRIKERS B13 in 1913, Equi was an outspoken opponent of United States entry into World War I, famously confronting Portland's 1916 Preparedness Day parade with a banner proclaiming "Down with Imperialism." On May Day 1916, Equi was selected as Oregon's representative to scatter Wobbly martyr JOE HILL'S B9 ashes (after his execution, his ashes were divided into forty-seven packets and one was sent to labor leaders in every state—except Utah, where he was murdered.) She was arrested many times in struggles over birth control, labor, and peace. Finally, as punishment for making an antiwar speech at the IWW Hall in June 1918, she was sentenced to three years in San Quentin State Prison, despite being defended by COLONEL CHARLES ERSKINE SCOTT (C. E. S.) WOOD B29. The federal government employed Margaret Lowell Paul as an informer against Equi during the Irish nationalist Kathleen O'Brennan's visit to Portland. In the Portland Hotel in August of 1918, Equi confronted U.S. military intelligence agents who were harassing O'Brennan. Equi was able to trigger a police raid on the hotel as a site of prostitution, telling the manager it was in retaliation for his cooperation with the intelligence agents.

Equi's longtime housemate at **1423 SW Hall Street**, Communist leader ELIZABETH GURLEY FLYNN C6, recalled the following: "Doctor [Equi] gets [liquor] from the police station…the big cops come sneaking up with it for her." In poor health, Equi left her bed for the first time in two years in July 1934 to take a check for $250 to striking longshoremen in order to assure their medical care. She adopted Mary Equi (1915–1998), who became the youngest female pilot in the Northwest in 1932 and later married the radical Joseph C. Lukes, a 1934 Reed College graduate. A play dramatizing the relations between Equi, Flynn, and Mary, *A Most Dangerous Woman* by Myra Donnelly, was produced at the Interstate Firehouse Cultural Center in Portland in 1995.

 Industrial Workers of the World

IWW, whose members were known as the Wobblies, was a dedicated enemy of capitalism and received significant support from workers who believed they should rule the world. Unlike the Socialist Party, the IWW expressed contempt for electoral politics. In Portland and throughout the Northwest, the IWW attracted loggers, miners, farmhands, and mill workers, renting its first Portland hall at 493 W. Burnside Street in 1907. They later moved to NW 2nd Avenue and Couch Street and then to 535 NW Davis Street—a site recently replaced by a fashionable condo. In March 1907, the IWW conducted its first major strike when one thousand six hundred men, organized by W. Y. Yarrow, struck the Eastern & Western Lumber Mill on the north waterfront of MacCormick Pier and the Inman-Poulsen Mill on the east side, between the Hawthorne and Ross Island Bridges. Three thousand sawmill workers walked out of the mills, demanding higher wages and shorter hours. The Wobblies called this "the first shot in the class war in the Northwest." Resurrected late in the twentieth century, the Wobblies have made several more recent attempts to organize gas stations, restaurants, child welfare centers, and the Reed College library in Portland. In 2006, their hall was at **311 N. Ivy Street**.

The Wobblies were a major target of reactionary vigilantes, local police, and the federal government. When Florence vigilantes kidnapped seven Wobblies in 1913, Governor Oswald D. West considered imposing martial law on the town. IWW members were also among the first victims of Oregon's notorious Criminal Syndicalism Act, which was Salem's answer to the Russian Revolution and became the legal foundation for the ensuing Red Scare. The law was first used by the Portland Police RED SQUAD F26 to arrest Wobbly Jay Wirth for selling the IWW newspaper on the street in 1919. On November 11, 1919, the WORKERS, SOLDIERS, AND SAILORS COUNCIL B31 was raided and fifty-six people, including twenty-six Wobblies, were arrested. Less than two months later, about thirty members of the Communist Labor Party (CLP)—which JOHN REED B20 had recently helped organize—were arrested. The twenty-six Wobblies and six of the CLP members were charged with violating the Criminal Syndicalism Act, which the CLP called the "Oregon Comical Silliyism Law," and about twelve received deportation warrants. William U'Ren defended three of the CLP members but one of them, writing from the Multnomah County Jail, complained that U'Ren had only read Tennyson poems to the jury, and "absolutely forgot to refute any of the accusations of the prosecution. In short, he sabotaged on us all the way through."[8]

The last Wobbly prosecuted under the act was Ole Hendricks, arrested in Tillamook in 1923 and defended by Portland progressive attorney BURL (B. A.) GREEN C22. Hendricks's trial ended in a hung jury, but the act was used against other radicals, mainly Communists such as BEN BOLOFF C3. This ended in 1938 when the U.S. Supreme Court freed Portland Communist leader DIRK DEJONGE C15 from prison.

In May of 1912, Wobblies organized a brief strike of five hundred tracklayers to protest the Portland Railway, Light, and Power Company's corrupt job-fee racket. In 1914, they invented the eat-in. Forty Wobblies entered Meves Restaurant at SW 6th Avenue and Washington Street, ordered bountiful meals, and told the cashier that Mayor Albee would pay for it. A crowd of five hundred watched from the sidewalk as twenty police arrived to remove the well-fed Wobblies, who were then sentenced to jail. The same day, fourteen Wobblies ate at Peerless Cafeteria, and the next day, seven ate steaks at another restaurant.

At the Spanish-American War Monument in LOWNSDALE SQUARE A7, the IWW held a free speech rally on the evening of July 17, 1913. This rally was attacked by angry veterans, who were deputized as specials by the city, and about twenty-five Wobblies were jailed. Their comrades then demonstrated before the neighboring Multnomah County Courthouse, demanding the release of fellow worker George Reece and other Wobblies.

 Ed Boyce

Ed Boyce, a leader of the Western Federation of Miners in Idaho and a supporter of the IWW B7 and Debs, moved to Portland in 1909 after retiring from union organizing. Here, he "became an avid reader of social

theory and Irish poetry" and lived quietly with his wife
Eleanor, "often passing the whole day sitting in the
same room reading." His wife Eleanor took an interest in art and became a member of the Portland Art
Association, and the family donated freely to a number
of local charities. In 1911, Boyce invested money in
the Portland Hotel, then located at the current site of
Pioneer Square and other local real estate and was
elected president of the Oregon Hotel Association in
1936. When he died in 1941, the former radical left an
estate of over $1 million, and perhaps that's why after
Boyce moved to Portland, Debs wrote that he had been
"virtually forgotten by the officials of the organization
he served at a time when it required real men to speak
out for labor."

 9 Joe Hill

In late 1910, the Wobbly organizer and song writer
Joe Hill wrote a letter to *The Industrial Worker*, the
IWW newspaper, identifying himself as a member of
the Portland Local, signing the first documented use
of the name (his Swedish name was Hillstrom) which
would later become known throughout the world. He
mentioned traveling through Pendleton and denounced
Portland police attacks on Wobblies and other workers
in the Portland area. Hill rose in the IWW organization and traveled widely, organizing workers under
the IWW banner, writing political songs and satirical
poems, and making speeches until he was murdered
by the state of Utah in 1919. One of his best-known
songs, "The Preacher and the Slave" (a parody of the
then well known hymn "In the Sweet Bye and Bye"),
was first introduced in Portland shortly after his letter
was published in 1910. Another Wobbly songmaster,
Harry "Haywire Mac" McClintock, recalls, "I first met
[Joe Hill] in Portland, Oregon, fall of 1910. He brought
'Preacher and the Slave' to the Portland IWW Hall."[9] It
has appeared in every edition of the IWW's *Little Red
Songbook* since 1911 as "Long-haired Preacher Man."

> Long-haired preachers come out every night,
> Try to tell you what's wrong and what's right;
> But when asked how 'bout something to eat
> They will answer with voices so sweet:
> You will eat, bye and bye
> In that glorious land above the sky;
> Work and pray,
> Live on hay,
> You'll get pie in the sky when you die

 March of the Unemployed 1914

On January 11, 1914, an "army of the unemployed" was joined by Wobblies and marched from Portland down the Willamette Valley. Oregon City's mayor let 125 marchers use its armory and fed them supper and breakfast. By contrast, the mayor of Woodburn organized a posse of several hundred men to keep the marchers from stopping in town. In **Salem** they camped outside Governor Oswald D. West's home. West was sympathetic, but he did not succeed in persuading the legislature to pass a public works bill. A few of the marchers got jobs through Salem churches, but more were arrested in the IWW's B7 restaurant "eat-in" and expelled from town. Albany's mayor ordered his fire department to threaten the Wobblies with fire hoses, but the march continued down to Eugene.

 Kathryn Seaman Beck

Kathryn (Kitty) Seaman Beck, described as a ward of Colonel C. E. S. Wood B29, was actually his lover. She was from a wealthy family and "at home in the world of literature, art, philosophy, and biography." She was Wood's secretary in his private office in room 419 of the Chamber of Commerce building, 525 SW 5th Avenue, and ran the Portland defense committee for the IWW leadership on trial for sedition in 1919. Observing the trial in Chicago, she met George Vanderveer, a prominent attorney who headed their defense and later opened a Legal Aid

Bureau in Portland. She became his close companion and later wife. Shortly after a visit from Wood to their home near Seattle in 1924, the unhappy and drinking Beck committed suicide by inhaling chloroform.[10] Dr Equi B6 accused Wood of being responsible.[11]

 12 The Catlin-Gabel School

The Catlin-Gabel School, today located at **8825 SW Barnes Road**, was founded in 1911 as Miss Catlin's School for Girls by Ruth Catlin (1883–1978) in a house on NW Irving Street. Committed to the "independence and freedom of action for women," her school drew its students largely from Portland's wealthy elite. She was later placed on a list of active communist sympathizers by the Portland Police Red Squad F26 because in 1936 she was a member of the Oregon Committee to Aid Spanish Democracy, which was devoted to defending the elected Spanish government against a fascist invasion. After leaving the school to a board of trustees in 1928, she "took up the cause of workers' rights…and debated with high-powered capitalists."

 13 Oregon Packing Company Strike 1913

The intersection of **SE 7th Avenue and Belmont Street** was the scene of the **1913 Oregon Packing Company Strike**, which was comprised of mainly women workers supported by the IWW B7 and other labor organizers. Dr Equi B6 and Tom Burns C19, among others, were radicalized by their support of the strike, which was also supported by Portlander Mary Schwab, a Socialist Party member and daughter-in-law of Chicago Haymarket defendant Michael Schwab. Lucy Parsons, widow of another defendant who was executed for the 1886 bomb attack that killed several policemen, visited Portland to support the strike and to speak at a downtown rally.

Will Daly

Everyone expected Portland labor leader and City Council member **Will Daly** (1869–1924) to be elected mayor in 1917. But a few days before the election, *The Oregonian* published on its front page his 1910 application for membership in the Socialist Party (stolen in a burglary the night before). Despite *The Oregonian's* red-baiting, George L. Baker beat Daly by less than two thousand of the forty-eight thousand votes cast, in one of the earliest elections in which women were allowed to vote (the first was Portland's 1913 municipal election). Daly first worked in Portland as a printer, and by 1908 was elected president of the Oregon Federation of Labor.[12] In that position, Daly introduced the IWW's leader, "Big Bill" Haywood, to thousands in a 1909 labor parade as "the man who has suffered more in the cause of organized labor than any other in the U.S.," expressing appreciation for the large socialist participation in the event. But after he was elected to the city council in 1911, at the urging of the Workingmen's Political Club, he began to distance himself from Socialism.

This did not prevent *The Oregonian* from leading a hysterical campaign against Daly, accusing him of supporting a general strike and asking, "Shall Portland be turned over to the radical labor agitator and the IWW?" Trumpeting his Socialist Party application, the paper tried to frighten its readers by warning, "If the people elect Daly, we shall have a Socialist for mayor." By 1920, Daly's socialist politics had degenerated to the extent that he endorsed Baker's reactionary administration.

 Sister Miriam Theresa

Sister Miriam Theresa (Caroline Gleason, 1886–1962), who co-founded the Catholic Women's League and the Oregon Consumer League, went on to become head of the Social Work department at what today is **Marylhurst University**, south of Portland. Although not an ideological radical, Gleason worked in Portland factories to gather data on the exploitation of women workers, leading to Oregon's enactment of the nation's first effective minimum wage law for women in 1912. As secretary of the Oregon Industrial Welfare Commission, she surveyed living conditions for women in Portland that resulted in a new city housing code. In 1916, she took vows and joined the Sisters of Holy Names and became Sister Miriam Theresa. She went on to become the first woman to receive a PhD from the Catholic University of America. In the tradition of progressive Catholic concern for the working class, she saw the minimum wage law as a means of industrial conciliation between the opposed interests of capital and labor.

 16 Louise Olivereau

Louise Olivereau (1884–1963) was associated with the Portland Modern School in 1912. An anarchist, poet, and teacher, she was a typist for the IWW in Seattle when she was convicted and jailed for more than two years (1917–1920) for opposing World War I. Right after her release from prison, she spoke at the 1920 May Day rally at Portland's FINNISH HALL F17 at *3425 N. Montana Avenue*.

 17 Roubaix de L'Abrie Richey

Roubaix de L'Abrie (Robo) Richey (1890–1922), artist and first husband of the celebrated photographer and Communist Tina Modotti (1896–1942), was born on a farm near Portland, attended Lincoln High School, and studied Spanish at the YMCA. In 1912, while living with his parents at *3158 SE 51st Avenue*, he published his first short story, "Webfoot" in the *Overland Monthly*. The story follows an army recruit from Oregon who kills a railroad worker during a strike and is in turn killed by the dead worker's enraged comrades. The dying webfoot laments, "he would never gaze upon Oregon ranges or the red Yamhill slopes down to the Willamette again." Richey later moved to San Francisco, where he met and married Modotti in 1918. While they lived in Los Angeles, Richey was a cartoonist and contributing editor for Gale's *International Journal for Revolutionary Communism*. The couple later moved to Mexico where Richey died of smallpox in 1922. His gravestone at the American cemetery in Mexico City is dedicated *from Modottias Su Esposa* (his wife).

 Grace De Graff

In 1915, **Grace De Graff** (1879–1951), principal of Kenton Elementary School, was one of forty-seven women led by the prominent social reformer Jane Adams, and the only delegate from the American West to attend the founding meeting of the **Women's International League for Peace and Freedom (WILPF)** at The Hague. The meeting was a call to women from around the world to "refuse to do the work men cannot do because they are busy murdering other men." According to her niece in Portland, De Graff "often revealed local scoundrels for what they were," and so "created quite a stir in her day and was not very popular." A lifelong activist and leader of teacher organizations, De Graff received Upton Sinclair, among others, at her home at **2312 SW Sheffield Avenue**. She issued an appeal "To the Teachers of the World" in 1916 that urged them "to teach the truth to the children under your care so that they may no longer be dazzled and blinded by the glittering lies of militarism." Her niece also recalled that De Graff "championed the cause of the socialist regime back in the thirties. She thought what the Russians were doing was a desirable state of affairs." But she also "thought Aaron Frank was the nicest man,"[13] and was able to persuade him to make generous donations to her project for Kenton's poor families. She was invited to the White House by Eleanor Roosevelt in 1932 and to Oregon Governor Douglas McKay's inauguration (he was one of her students) in 1949. Her favorite peace organization, WILPF, continues to be active in Portland with offices at 1819 NW Everett Street.

 Louise Bryant

The celebrated radical writer **Louise Bryant** (1887–1936) lived with her first husband, dentist Paul Trullinger, in a houseboat at the Oregon Yacht Club, and maintained a studio in today's Professional Building at *1021 SW Yamhill Street*. They later lived at *2226 NE 53rd Avenue* as well as *11801 SW Riverwood Road*. She met JOHN REED B20 during his visit to Portland in December 1915 and left her husband and Portland to live with (and eventually marry) him in New York. Bryant considered Portland "a silly old town" because "it had [Reed's] presence here for weeks without appreciating it."[14] For his part, Reed "couldn't imagine" how Bryant could have "grown into an artist, a poet, and a revolutionary" in "this infertile soil, this spiritual vacuum." Bryant returned to Portland only once, in 1919. Before four thousand people in a new Civic Auditorium (today's Keller Auditorium, renovated in 1968) she demanded the immediate withdrawal of U.S. troops from Siberia, sent by President Wilson to unsuccessfully (in Winston Churchill's words) "strangle the Russian Revolution in its cradle." *The Oregonian* noted that she "flourished a red cape that dared Portland to imagine her political beliefs" but that, otherwise, "Louise has changed little. Aside from her George Sand haircut, she is the same little radicalist and vigorous performer that left Portland three years ago." She is buried in Paris.

 20 John Reed

Probably the best known of Portland radicals is the writer, poet, and revolutionary **John Reed** (1886–1920). All that remains of the big house on the hill above the city where he was born are the steps linking the end of *SW Cedar Street with the end of SW Cactus Drive*. He remembered Cedar Hill as a "lordly grey mansion modeled on a French chateau, with its immense park, its formal gardens, lawns, stables, greenhouses, and glass grape arbor, the tame deer among the trees." Reed's first published work was featured in the May 1902 issue of *The Troubadour*, the student literary magazine of his private high school, the Portland Academy. The final stanza of the poem describes the eighteenth century eruption of Mt. St. Helens and its impact on the Columbia River, written when Jack Reed (as he signed himself) was fifteen years old:

Thus it was the tribe of Clatsops,
In the dawn of living beings,
Was swept almost from existence.
But across that deep, dark valley,
Flows a river, broad and lovely.
To the east the Smoking Mountain
Robed in Liao's snowy blanket
Rises smokeless now to heaven,
Covered with eternal whiteness

Home for the summer of 1909 from Harvard, a sarcastic Reed wrote a girlfriend asking if "Portland [was] still the same giddy bewildering place that [made] people leave New York in the gay season and come out here for fun." Visiting on the death of his father in 1912, Reed predicted he'd "go mad in a year" if he had to live here. On his last visit to his hometown in December 1915, Reed found it "awful beyond words...I don't feel I can talk to a single person here." Reed died of typhus in the Soviet Union after publishing *Ten Days That Shook the World* and remains buried in the revolutionaries' cemetery at the walls of the Kremlin.

To celebrate May Day 2001, the Oregon Cultural Heritage Commission dedicated a bench in memory of Reed overlooking his birthplace near the entrance to Washington Park.

 ### 21 Carl & Helen Walters

A Portland couple, **Carl and Helen Walters**,[15] were JOHN REED'S B20 and COLONEL C. E. S. WOOD'S B29 favorite local artists, as well as LOUISE BRYANT'S B19 closest friends in 1915. Reed and Bryant's first date was at dinner at the Walters' studio in the former Labbe building at **SW 1st Avenue and Washington Street**. Carl was, like Louise, a subscription agent for the radical monthly, *The Masses*. The Walterses moved to New York in 1919, where Carl became a prominent ceramicist.

 22 Emma Goldman & Ben Reitman

In August of 1915, famed radicals **Emma Goldman** and **Ben Reitman** were arrested in Portland for distributing literature on the subject of birth control just as they began a lecture on the topic. Goldman was released on $500 bail provided by C. E. S. WOOD B29 and after the police chief proclaimed she would not speak in Portland again, she announced that she would try to speak on the subject of birth control the next day, but Dr. Reitman remained in jail. Goldman and Reitman were convicted and fined $100 on the birth control charge, and when Goldman spoke at TURN VEREIN HALL F17, which stood on the northeast corner of *SW 4th Avenue and Yamhill Street*, the topic was changed to "The Intermediate Sex (A Discussion of Homosexuality)." The audience included plainclothes police, a deputy district attorney, and a deputy city attorney but she was not arrested on that occasion. She also presented additional lectures, including "The Sham of Culture" at the Portland Public Library to an overflowing crowd. Eventually, Goldman's case was dismissed by Portland Circuit Judge William Gatens who concluded, "There is too much tendency to prudery nowadays."

23 Beatrice Morrow Cannady

A few years after **Beatrice Morrow Cannady** arrived in Portland in 1912, she organized one of the city's first interracial protest events: a movement to ban the nation's favorite, but racist, Ku Klux Klan recruiting film, *Birth of a Nation*. Enthusiastically endorsed by President Woodrow Wilson, the silent movie was credited with helping the Oregon Klan grow into a major political force. When it was shown at the singularly named Blue Mouse Theater at *SW 11th Avenue and Washington Street*, its owner John Hamrick used the occasion to announce his Klan membership.[16] According to Portland civil rights activist Bobbie Nunn, the film was eventually banned in Portland in the 1950s after an effort headed by the National Association for the Advancement of Colored People (NAACP) and the Urban League.[17]

Beatrice moved to Portland to marry Edward D. Cannady and to work with him on the four-page weekly, *Advocate*, which Cannady founded in 1903 with other Portland Hotel employees. The Cannadys and their two sons lived at **2516 NE 26th Avenue**. Beatrice became secretary of the new NAACP, organized in 1913 (the oldest continuously organized chapter west of the Mississippi) and fought discrimination and segregation in the community and the courts. In 1922, she became the first black woman to graduate from law school, attending night classes at the Northwest College of Law. Although she represented clients in court, she did not pass the Oregon Bar examination. After failing to be elected to the state legislature, she left Portland for good in 1936 and lived in California for the rest of her life.

 24 Gipsy Smith Tabernacle

The Gipsy Smith Tabernacle, which stood on the northeast corner of **SW 12th Avenue and Morrison Street**, was named for a British evangelist and became a shelter for Portland's homeless in 1913. In that year, the Unemployed League drew nine thousand people to a rally in the Plaza Blocks demanding the city meet at least some of their desperate needs. As Louise Bryant B19 wrote in *The Masses*, "men slept by the hundreds in the breezy tabernacle built for Gypsy [sic] Smith's revival meetings."[18] The men elected their own committee to run the "bunkhouse," including a barbershop and shoe repair, and negotiated with city and charity officials. By 1915, businessmen demanded the shelter close, saying: "it has become known throughout the Northwest that Portland has become a 'soft place' for the 'riffraff' of Seattle, Tacoma, and other Northwestern cities." Despite Edward Gilbert's declaration that the men of the Unemployed League wanted "work and not charity," the city closed the building a few months later. As Gilbert later told a public hearing, some food and shelter were provided, but he maintained, it wasn't a solution "to the unemployed problem."[19]

In 1917, Roy Ott and George Dunmire, who organized the **American Federation of Labor (AFL) Papermaker's Union** at the Crown Willamette and Hawley Mills in suburban West Linn, were fired for union activities. Their fellow workers went on strike in protest. The mills were closed, but the owners brought in scabs (today, employers call them replacement workers), and the strike continued with widespread community support for over a year. Crown's manager B. F. McBain even built a hotel, The Swan, to house the non-union workers. It inspired this anonymous poem (credited to a six-year-old girl), which was published in the *Oregon City Morning Enterprise* on November 20, 1917:

> Hotel de Swan
> If McBain could break the unions here
> It would fill his heart with joy,
> He ne'er would hire those scabs again
> To work in his employ.
> He sets up good grub in the "Hotel de Swan"
> To keep their spirits gay
> But just the same the unions here
> Are on the strike to stay.

On June 23, 1918, a bloody confrontation between hundreds of scabs and strikers took place at the **Oregon City** end of the suspension bridge at **7th and Main Streets**. Kelley Loe of the *Oregon Labor Press* witnessed the battle, at which the local police, reportedly sympathetic to the strikers, were conspicuously absent. The strikers declared victory, but local business leaders demanded a coat of tar and feather for the union heads and the state Federation of Labor, who they called "Bolsheviki and riffraff." Eventually, the strike was broken and the mills were not unionized again until 1937. The "Hotel de Swan" became the West Linn Inn until it was demolished in 1985. The last mill in Oregon City closed in 1996.

 **Hazel Hall**

Poet **Hazel Hall** (1886–1924) was confined to a wheel-chair for most of her short life and worked from the top floor of her family's house at **106 NW 22nd Place**, where the Oregon Cultural Heritage Commission has placed a memorial. She is also honored on the sidewalk at Trimet's PGE Park MAX stop.

Hall published some of her work in the New York radical journal, *The Masses*, where JOHN REED B20 was an editor. The journal also published Portlanders C. E. S. WOOD B29 and LOUISE BRYANT B19. This poem, reminding us she was a seamstress, appeared in *The Masses* in 1917:

> Needle, running in and out,
> In and out, in and out,
> Do you know what you're about,
> In and out, in and out?
> Fingers, going to and fro,
> To and fro, to and fro,
> Do you know the path you go,
> To and fro, to and fro?
> I might tell you why you're taking
> Such good stitches: You are making
> Out of linen fine as breaking
> Ocean-spray upon a bluff,
> Pleating for a Bishop's cuff!
> I might make you understand
> That a Bishop's white, white hand,
> Because of you, will be more fair,
> Will be raised in better prayer.
> Even then you, would you know
> Why you're going to and fro?
> Would you doubt what you're about,
> Running in and running out?

 Wesley Everest & the Centralia Massacre

Wesley Everest (1890–1919), the Wobbly and World War I veteran who was infamously lynched in the **Centralia Massacre** on Armistice Day 1919, was born in Newberg

and grew up on his aunt's Westfall dairy near Portland.
In 1914, he was captured in Coos County by a three
hundred-strong vigilante gang of local businessmen and
run out of town with other labor organizers. His grave
in the Sticklin-Greenwood Memorial Park cemetery in
Centralia, Washington, was unmarked until the late 1930s.
Old-timers located it in the southwest corner and the
IWW erected a headstone.

 Oregon Socialist Party

In 1919, the **Oregon Socialist Party** was led by Harlin Tal-
bert with offices at *529 SW 2nd Avenue*, where he edited
the *Oregon Socialist Party Bulletin*. In Portland the party had
seven locals, which comprised over half of its two thousand members in the state. The largest was its West Side
or "American" Local with 427 members, followed by the
Scandinavian (300), Finnish (141), East Side "American"
(101), German (75), Lettish (37), and Estonian (30).

 Colonel C. E. S. Wood

Colonel C. E. S. Wood (1852–1944) was a military official
and radical lawyer who defended, among others, Dr. Marie
D. Equi B6. He was also a dominant figure in Portland's civic
and cultural life at the turn of the century until he moved
to California in 1919. He supported local radicals like
Equi, visitors like Emma Goldman B22 and Margaret Sanger,
and mentored others like John Reed B20. A friend of the
dispossessed Chief Joseph of the Nez Perce, he sent his
son Erskine Wood to spend summers with the Chief. All
that remains of Wood's Portland home is the low brick
balustrade along the patio of the Portland Garden Club
at *1132 SW Vista Avenue*. His son's house, the Erskine
Wood House, is at *2229 SW King Court*.

 Louise Hunt

During World War II, **Louise Hunt** (1876–1960) was
the assistant to Miss Mary Frances Isom, the Portland
Library's head librarian who had recently moved into

a new building on **SW 10th Avenue**.[20] A committed
pacifist at a time when a Methodist minister was urging
the Portland Rotarians "if you have a pacifist, shoot
him," she became a victim of Portland's World War I Red
Scare in 1918 for refusing to buy war bonds. Although
initially supported by the Library Board, its members
caved before a flood of criticism from Portland power
brokers and effectively fired her. The witch hunt against
Portlanders accused of having a lack of enthusiasm for
the war also cost Nell Moran, a Portland school teacher,
her job and put DR. MARIE EQUI B6, Henry Albers of Albers
Milling Company, and Floyd Ramp of Eugene in jail.

 31 The Workers, Soliders, and Sailors Council

The Workers, Soldiers, and Sailors Council of Portland, which was inspired by the Soviets ("councils" in
Russian) of the Russian Revolution, was organized by
local radicals in January 1919 at Arion Hall. This building
stood at **SW Oak Street and 2nd Avenue** until it was
replaced by Portland Police Bureau Headquarters, and
eventually became an office building.

The Council's organizer was Harry M. Wicks (1889–
1956), the editor of the *Western Socialist* who had run
for Congress on the Socialist Party ticket in 1918. The
Council was organized to bring newly discharged servicemen together with unions in a new radical political
movement. One of the Council's actions was to organize
six hundred men in the Plaza Blocks to protest DR. MARIE
D. EQUI'S B6 sentencing to prison in 1918. Replaced as
council president by a foundry workers' union member,
Wicks left the Council, and it dissolved after about six
months. Wicks later became a Communist Party leader
in the east and accompanied James W. Ford, the Party's
black vice-presidential candidate, to Portland in 1932.

 32 The Portland Labor College

The Portland Labor College, sponsored by the Central
Labor Council and located in the Labor Temple at **SW
4th and Jefferson Street**, existed from 1921 to 1927,[21]

and was briefly revived in the 1970s see F4. Its early life reflected tension between the radicals drawn to it and its sponsorship by the more conservative AFL craft unions. Its main organizer was Joseph Schwartrauler, head of the history department and the Portland Teachers Union at Lincoln High School. Its teachers included Charles McKinley of Reed College (later president of the American Political Science Association) and radical Ray Neufer of the carpenters union and Works Progress Administration's (WPA) furniture designer fame. The late Aaron Director, a student of Schwartrauler who, after graduating from Yale, became Labor College director in 1924, invited ELIZABETH GURLEY FLYNN C6, Scott Nearing, and other radicals to lecture at its forum. This soured his relations with the Central Labor Council and he left Portland for a long and increasingly conservative career as an economist at the University of Chicago. There he studied with future Illinois Senator Paul Douglas, who taught at Reed from 1916 to 1917. Director invited his sister Rose, who attended Reed to become a graduate economics student at the University of Chicago, where she met and married the late Nobel Prize winner Milton Friedman. In 1922, at the initiative of the Portland Teachers Union, the Labor College established the Portland Labor Players, the first and only workers' theater in the nation. The Players were under the direction of Doris Smith.

 33 The Homemade Portland Revolution

Hoping for a general strike called **The Homemade Portland Revolution**, Portland Wobblies called a longshoremen strike in 1922 that was expanded to streetcar conductors. The strike incurred the wrath of the reactionary Mayor George L. Baker (1917–1933), a violent enemy of unions who had directed police raids against radicals during the first Red Scare several years earlier. Backed by the influential Ku Klux Klan of Portland and most businessmen, Baker threw four hundred strikers into Rocky Butte jail. One of them, "Dublin Dan" Liston, used the time to write "The Portland Revolution," a song reprinted ever since in the IWW's *Little Red Songbook*. Its first verse goes:

> The Revolution started, so the judge informed the Mayor,
> Now Baker paces back and forth, and raves and pulls his hair,
> The waterfront is tied up tight, the Portland newsboy howls,
> And not a thing is moving, only Mayor Baker's bowels.

Frank T. Johns

Portland's only presidential candidate, **Frank T. Johns**, was the nominee of the SLP in 1924 and 1928. He was a member of Carpenters Union Local 226, which merged into today's Local 247, at **2215 NE Lombard Street**. Johns received about one thousand votes in Oregon and thirty-six thousand nation-wide in 1924, but on May 20, 1928, only weeks after his nomination, he died after a campaign speech on the banks of the Deschutes River in Bend. As the private memorial erected in 1970 relates, Johns dove into the river in a vain attempt to save a drowning boy and drowned in the effort. His Portland Carpenters' Union Local declared that their brother "had devoted his life to the working class" and died a hero but they noted that the majority of his union's members "did not agree with his political theories."

Pacific Coast Workers Summer School

In 1928, four students from Portland (and another eight from Astoria, Eugene, Clatskanie, Knappa, Marshfield, and Hood River) graduated from the **Communist Party's Pacific Coast Workers Summer School** in nearby Woodland, Washington. Portlanders Helen Harila, Eva Yank, and Alma Reinis were among the students at the school that summer who infiltrated a National Guard dance in Vancouver, Washington, to distribute anti-militarist pamphlets to their dancing partners. Henry Routu was the other Portland graduate.

1 For more information about current Socialist Party Multnomah County Local meeting times visit: http://www.thesocialistparty. org/spo/pdx.

2. John Terry, *The Oregonian*, November 20, 2005.

3. Andrew Nils Bryans. "The Response to Left-Wing Radicalism in Portland, Oregon, from 1917 to 1941."(Unpublished M.A. Thesis, Portland State University, 2002).

4. William Z. Foster, *From Bryan to Stalin* (New York: International Publishers, 1937) 27.

5. William Z. Foster, *From Bryan to Stalin* (New York: International Publishers, 1937); E.P. Johanningsmeier, *Forging American Communism: The Life of William Z. Foster* (Princeton: Princeton University Press, 1994).

6. *The Oregonian*, March 25, 1905.

7. Tim Hills, "Myths and Anarchists: Sorting Out the History of Portland's White Eagle Saloon," *Oregon Historical Quarterly*, Winter 2000.

8. K. W. Oster, "The Class War in Oregon," *The Toiler* (Cleveland) May 7, 1920.

9. *Don't Mourn—Organize: Songs of Labor Organizer Joe Hill*, Smithsonian Folkways CD 40026.

10. Lowell S. Hawley and Ralph Busnell Potts, *Counsel For the Damned: A Biography of George Francis Vanderveer* (J.B. Lippincott Co; 1st ed edition, 1953), esp. p 237–8, 271–2, 297–8.

11. Robert Hamburger, *Two Rooms: The Life of Charles Erskine Scott Wood* (Lincoln, NE.: University of Nebraska Press, 1998).

12. Robert D. Johnston, "The Myth of the Harmonious City: Will Daly, Lora Little and the Hidden Face of Progressive-Era Portland," *Oregon Historical Quarterly*, Fall 1998.

13. Dorothy Reeves Wiley and Grace De Graff, undated typescript. Author's collection.

14. Michael Munk, "The Portland Years of John Reed and Louise Bryant" (Portland, OR: Oregon Cultural Heritage Commission, 3rd edition, 2003).

15. Michael Munk, "The 'Portland Period' of Artist Carl Walters," *Oregon Historical Quarterly*, Summer 2000; Munk, "The Diaries of Helen Lawrence Walters," *Oregon Historical Quarterly*, Winter 2005.

16. Kimberly Mangun, "As Citizens of Portland, We Must Protest:

Beatrice Morrow Cannady and the African-American Response to D. W. Griffith's 'Masterpiece' *Oregon Historical Quarterly,* Fall 2006.

17. "Lifelong activist ready to talk race," *The Oregonian*, December 11, 1997.

18. "Two Judges," *The Masses,* April 1916.

19. Dimitri Palmateer, "Charity and the 'Tramp': Itinerancy, Unemployment, and Municipal Government from Coxey to the Unemployed league" *Oregon Historical Quarterly*, Summer 2006.

20. Annette Bartholomae,. "A Conscientious Objector: Oregon, 1918," *Oregon Historical Quarterly*, September 1970.

21. Jerry Lembcke, "Labor and Education: The Portland Labor College, 1921–1929," *Oregon Historical Quarterly*, Summer 1984.

B: 1900 –1930
Wobblies & Socialists

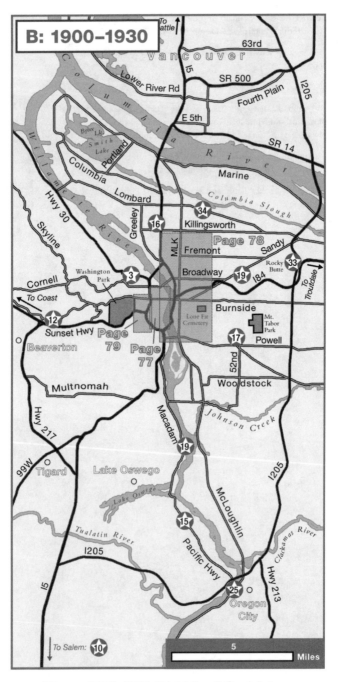

B: 1900–1930

To Seattle

Vancouver

63rd

SR 500

Fourth Plain

I205

I5

Lower River Rd

E 5th

SR 14

Columbia River

Bybee Lk.

Smith Lake

Portland

Columbia

Lombard

Marine

Columbia Slough

Greeley

Willamette River

Hwy 30

Skyline

16

34

Killingsworth

MLK

Fremont

Page 78

Sandy

Cornell

Washington Park

3

Broadway

19

184

Rocky Butte

33

To Troutdale

To Coast

12

Sunset Hwy

Page 79

Page 77

Lone Fir Cemetery

Burnside

17

Mt. Tabor Park

Powell

52nd

Beaverton

Multnomah

Woodstock

Hwy 217

Macadam

19

Johnson Creek

I205

99W

Tigard

Lake Oswego

Lake Oswego

15

McLoughlin

Clackamas River

Tualatin River

I205

Pacific Hwy

Hwy 213

I5

25

Oregon City

To Salem

10

5

Miles

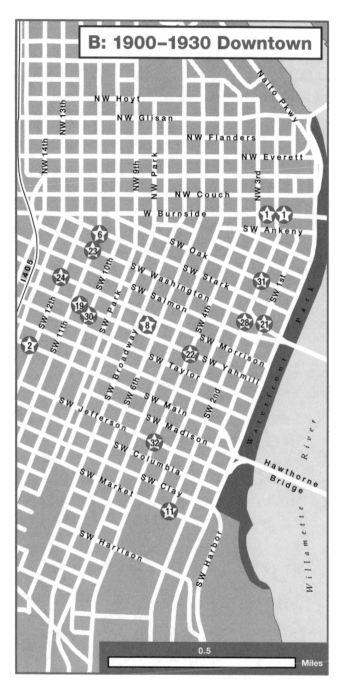

B: 1900–1930 Downtown

NW Hoyt
NW Glisan
NW Flanders
NW Everett
NW Couch
W Burnside

NW 14th
NW 13th
NW 9th
NW Park
NW 3rd

I405

SW Ankeny
SW Oak
SW Stark
SW Washington
SW Salmon
SW Morrison
SW Yamhill
SW Taylor
SW Main
SW Madison
SW Columbia
SW Clay
SW Market
SW Harrison
SW Jefferson

SW 10th
SW 12th
SW 11th
SW Park
SW Broadway
SW 6th
SW 4th
SW 2nd
SW Harbor

Naito Pkwy

Waterfront park

Hawthorne Bridge

Willamette River

0.5
Miles

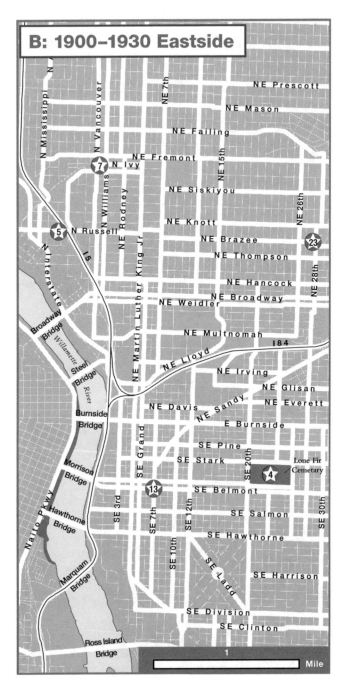

B: 1900–1930 Eastside

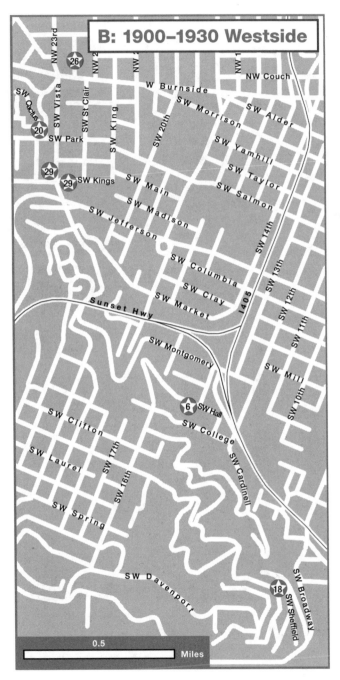

B: 1900–1930 Westside

NW 23rd
NW 2
NW 2
NW 1
NW Couch

SW Cactus
SW Vista
SW St Clair
SW King
SW 20th

W Burnside
SW Morrison
SW Alder
SW Yamhill
SW Taylor
SW Salmon

SW Park

SW Kings
SW Main
SW Madison
SW Jefferson
SW Columbia
SW Clay
SW Market

SW 14th
SW 13th
I405
SW 12th
SW 11th

Sunset Hwy

SW Montgomery

SW Mill

SW Hall
SW College
SW 10th

SW Clifton
SW 17th
SW 16th
SW Laurel
SW Cardinell

SW Spring

SW Davenport

SW Broadway
SW Sheffield

26 20 29 29 6 18

0.5
Miles

ERICKSON'S SALOON

Erickson's fame spread around the world, as sailors
carried word of its 16-ounce nickel beer (hard drinks
two for a quarter), its free meal of gargantuan
proportions (as long as you kept drinking), its bar 684
feet in length and its delightful lady performers in the
Cabaret Grill. Loggers, farm hands and other robust
working men came to Erickson's, some to spend
their stakes in one night revelries,
buying drinks all around.

The powerful and elite of Portland also came to
Erickson's. The balcony afforded those of wealth a
better view of the stage and of the "sea of life"
undulating below.

On the top floor there were cardrooms and cribs—
small cubicle-like rooms on either side of the hall—
for entertainments of a more private kind.

Top: Erickson's Saloon was a favorite of William Z. Foster, labor
leader and longtime head of the U.S Communist Party. *Colin Smith*.
Bottom: The plaque on the building that once housed Erickson's
reads: "Loggers, farm hands, and other robust working men came to
Erickson's some to spend their stakes in one night revelries, buying
drinks all around." *Colin Smith*.

The White Eagle Saloon, now owned by local restaurant chain McMenamin's, was named for the Polish national symbol. It hosted the radical Polish group Progress in rooms upstairs. *McMenamin's.*

Industrial Unionism

BY

WM. Z. FOSTER

5¢

This pamphlet of Foster's on Industrial Unionism, published in 1936, sold for five cents. *Oregon Historical Society, PAM 331.88 F758i.*

Dr. Marie D. Equi was one of the first women to graduate from the University of Oregon Medical School in 1903. She also fought militantly for workers' and women's rights. *Oregon Historical Society, OrHi60822.*

Dr. Marie D. Equi, as created by Icky A. *Icky A.*

 The house where Dr. Marie D. Equi lived with Elizabeth Gurley Flynn C6 is located at 1423 SW Hall Street. *Colin Smith.*

 This building at NW 3rd Avenue and Burnside Street served as headquarters for the IWW during the early years of the organization's life in Portland. *City of Portland Archives, A2000-033.*

Education ★ Organization ★ Emancipation

Knowledge, like energy, is power only when it is put to work to get results.

All together, the working class knows how to make everything, how to do everything, how to create abundance and the necessary conditions for happiness for us all. But to put that knowledge to work requires organization. To get the full results that can come only from using all of it, requires organization as a class—One Big Union.

Science is knowledge organized. The I. W. W. is the working class organized—just the working class, with everybody from the coal miner to the chemist who figures out how to make a new flavoring extract out of the coal, organized to use our brains for ourselves. And it spells emancipation and a new era of abundance and security.

To start the process takes scientific industrial union education—such as you spread when you get new readers for the I. W. W. periodicals and pamphlets, pass-out I. W. W. leaflets, or put up I. W. W. stickers. Educate to organize, and organize to educate—that's the road ahead to freedom. That's where the I.W.W. is marching, and you are cordially asked to hop into the parade.

 This IWW poster's heading, "Education—Organization—Emancipation" represents the most basic strategy used by the IWW in their struggle to give power to the "working class," whom they tried to form into "one big union." *Oregon Historical Society, OrHi77730.*

PORTLAND IWW PRESENTS
RADICAL BOOK FAIR
TWO TIL SEVEN
&
JOE HILL NIGHT
SEVEN TIL HALF PAST NINE
SUN. NOV.
19
AT
MUSIC BY   LIBERTY HALL
GENERAL STRIKE
& THE JOE HILLBILLIES   311
BOOKS BY   NORTH
LAUGHING HORSE,
IN OTHER WORDS,MICROCOSM,   IVY
CHARLES.H. KERR, BLACK ROSE
AND MANY MORE

9 Joe Hill Night is Portland's tribute to the IWW songwriter and the labor movement he represented. This flier advertised the 2006 version of this party, which was held at Liberty Hall in North Portland. There was a radical book fair and music from local radical bands. *Portland IWW.*

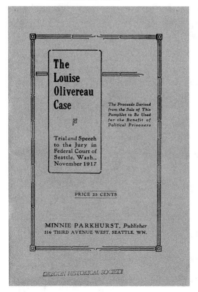

The
Louise
Olivereau
Case

The Proceeds Derived from the Sale of This Pamphlet to Be Used for the Benefit of Political Prisoners

Trial and Speech to the Jury in Federal Court of Seattle, Wash., November 1917

PRICE 25 CENTS

MINNIE PARKHURST, *Publisher*
316 THIRD AVENUE WEST, SEATTLE, WN.

OREGON HISTORICAL SOCIETY

16 This pamphlet tells the story of Louise Olivereau's trial in 1917. She was tried for her opposition to World War I. *Oregon Historical Society, PAM 323.4 P246L.*

 Louise Bryant lived with her first husband, Portland dentist Paul Trullinger, in this house at 2226 NE 53rd Avenue. *Colin White.*

 Bryant, right, is shown here in Portland circa 1912. Kina McKelvey, left, was a friend. *Larry Armstrong.*

 All that remains of John Reed's birthplace are the stone steps linking SW Cactus Drive with SW Cedar Street. This photo shows Reed's house as it looked while owned by his grandparents, Mr. and Mrs. H. Green. *Oregon Historical Society, OrHi80890.*

 The John Reed Memorial Bench can be found in Portland's Washington Park. This poster advertised the dedication of that bench in 2001. *Oregon Cultural Heritage Commission.*

29 Top: Colonel C. E. S. Wood supported local radicals like Emma Goldman B22, Margaret Sanger, and Dr. Marie D. Equi B6. He also served as a mentor to John Reed B20. *Oregon Historical Society, OrHi23607.*
Right: Colonel C. E. S. Wood as depicted on the front cover by Icky A. *Icky A.*

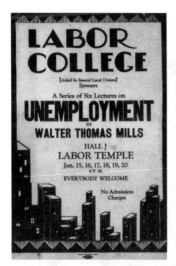

 Left: This poster advertises a series of lectures at the Portland Labor College, *A Series of Six Lectures on Unemployment,* by Walter Thomas Mills. *Norm Diamond.*

Right: This handbill from the Portland Labor Players II F4 is designed like a labor newspaper, complete with articles and ads. The handbill is from the play *1934: Blood and Roses. Norm Diamond.*

 Frank T. Johns was the only presidential candidate to come from Portland. After giving a campaign speech in Bend, Oregon, Johns dived into the Deschutes River to save two boys from drowning. He died in the attempt. This memorial was erected in 1970. *Michael Munk.*

Future Senator Richard Neuberger spoke to Reed College students at a 1938 peace rally on the Reed campus. He debated against war preparations, while his opponent, Oscar Gass, looked on. *Reed College Archives.*

C: 1930s
Unions & Commies

Portland joined in the surge of American radicalism during the Great Depression of the 1930s. Its major expression was the Communist Party, but the movement also included many other Americans who had decided that laissez faire capitalism was the cause of intolerable human suffering and exploitation. The Communist Party's work organizing much of the urban working class into the mass unions of the new Congress of Industrial Organizations (CIO) was its major achievement. This organizing was much more effective than its electoral politics, which mainly supported President Franklin Roosevelt and his New Deal Democrats. In 1932, the Communists' leader, former Portlander WILLIAM Z. FOSTER B1 drew only 1,618 votes from Oregonians in the Party's only presidential challenge of the decade.

Portland's most dramatic event of this period was its working class participation in the great WEST COAST MARITIME STRIKE OF 1934 C9, in which thousands united to win union recognition and eventual control of waterfront hiring. The victory came despite the city elite's hiring of vigilantes, as well as BLOODY WEDNESDAY AT TERMINAL FOUR C9 when police shot and wounded striking longshoremen. The strike is still commemorated every July 5 in Oaks Park by area International Longshore and Warehouse Union (ILWU) Locals, including Portland Local 8 and its young Local 5, which represents workers at Powell's Books.

Both the ILWU and the former Portland-headquartered International Woodworkers of America (IWA) were founded in the heyday of CIO organizing, as was the OREGON WORKERS ALLIANCE (OWA) C24. The OWA included not only New Deal public works and construction workers, but also radical artists and craftspeople supported

by the federal Works Progress Administration (WPA)
such as the Runquist brothers and MARTINA GANGLE CURL
F13. The painter Louis Bunce, whose once-controversial
mural still graces Portland International Airport, was
secretary of the Oregon office of the Federal Arts League.
It was located in the same office in the McKay Building, which was previously occupied by the International
Labor Defense (ILD). Bunce assisted on a WPA mural
that can be seen at 8720 N. Ivanhoe Street. Formerly the
St. Johns Post Office, it is now a Bahai Temple. Art community leaders who served on the Oregon committee
included Reed professors Barry Cerf, V. L. O. Chittick,
LLOYD REYNOLDS D32, and JESSIE M. SHORT C34, as well as artists
Virginia Darcey, DEAN WILLIAM GIVLER D35, and playwright
DAWN LOVELACE C16.

The Oregon Public Theater and art centers in Portland, La Grande (where MINOR WHITE C30 taught), Gold
Beach, and Salem (where Bunce taught) provided both
employment and cultural education to the Depression
era public. Many of Oregon's landmarks, such as Bonneville Dam (whose administrators hired WOODY GUTHRIE
D2 to write songs about it) and Timberline Lodge were
built as part of the federal government's response to
provide jobs to the unemployed in the economic crisis,
a response partly reflecting demands from the revived
radical movement. WPA workers divided into five-man
crews hauling carts and distributing ninety thousand
black and white ceramic numbers that still mark many
homes around the city. On the political front, the OREGON
COMMONWEALTH FEDERATION (OCF) C25 offered a common
home to radicals and liberals who shared the political
goal of electing New Deal Democrats and defeating
anti-Roosevelt conservatives in Oregon elections.

May Day became a major event for the Portland leftists in the 1930s. Formally known as "The International
Day of the Working Class," it was originally observed
locally by the Socialist Party. Before World War I and
through the 1930s, events took place at today's LOWNSDALE
SQUARE A7 (then called Plaza Park) at SW Main Street
between 3rd and 4th Avenues.

May Day 1934 was especially dramatic; it dawned with a large red flag flying proudly over city hall. Demonstrators gathering at the nearby square were delighted that the flag remained most of the day due to a "malfunctioning" pole mechanism that defeated Mayor Joe Carson's efforts to remove it. The Portland section of the Communist Party proudly announced that the parade, which was dedicated against "hunger, fascism, and war," would use a "technological advance"—a public address system—for the first time in Portland. The Unemployed Councils, organized by the Communist Party, called on all working class organizations (and sympathizers) to march to Plaza Park to demand unemployment insurance and social security, free milk for children, "more and better relief," and the "release of all class war prisoners."

In 1938, the United Front May Day Committee organized a rally in the Civic Auditorium (now Keller Auditorium) to aid the Spanish Republic, which was then under fascist attack. Police RED SQUAD F26 spies reported that this was "a complete change in tactics as experienced in former years when parades and soap boxing were the main events of May Day." Radicals returned to the Plaza Park Blocks for May Day 1939, when the Portland May Day Action Committee reminded the public that the tradition grew from an 1886 Chicago demonstration for the eight-hour day. The marchers called for labor unity, WPA jobs, and social security, urging the public to back President Roosevelt.

 Paul Siro

Paul Siro (1911–1932) was dubbed Astoria's Boy Communist when, at fourteen, he was elected student body president at Robert Gray Junior High School and was quickly expelled for wearing a Lenin button to class. Siro was active in the Communist Party in Portland until May 1932, when he disappeared from his home at **785 N. Minnesota Avenue** and was found dead in the Columbia River. His death remains a mystery and his headstone in Castle Rock's Hubbard-Whittle Cemetery reads:

Paul Siro
1911–1932
Our Comrade

 ## The Bonus Army

In a movement that began in Portland, tens of thousands of World War I veterans joined **The Bonus Army** in 1932 to march on Washington, D.C., and demand payment of promised bonuses. The Bonus Army started when three hundred men, led by former Army Sergeant Walter W. Waters (1898–1959), assembled at the Union Pacific railroad yards just north of the Broadway Bridge under a banner that read "Portland Bonus March—On to Washington." The vets, desperate because of the Depression, boarded a livestock train heading east. Waters, who was born in Burns, Oregon, was a superintendent at the Pacific Coast Fruit Company in Portland when the Depression cost him his job. At the Portland convention of the National Veterans Association that year, he proposed "every man present hop a freight and head for Washington to get the money that was rightfully theirs."[1]

Several months later, the veterans calling themselves The Bonus Expeditionary Force were on their way in cattle cars from Portland. As the news spread, contingents organized around the nation. Eventually as many as twenty-five thousand veterans set up an encampment at a Washington "Hooverville," a tent and shack refuge duplicated in every American city (including Portland) during the Depression. They elected Waters their Commander-in-chief and vowed to stay until Congress appropriated the bonus money. They were denounced as Reds and savagely attacked by U.S. Army troops under the command of General Douglas MacArthur, and aides Majors Dwight D. Eisenhower and George Patton. The Army burned the tent city, caused one hundred casualties, and routed the vets. Waters later got a federal job in Washington and led no more protests.

3 Ben Boloff

Ben Boloff (1893–1932), a Communist ditch digger, is buried in River View Cemetery, at **8421 SW Macadam Avenue**. He lies together with members of prominent Portland families, including the Corbetts, Failings, Dolphs, Couches, Skidmores, Terwilligers, Cornells, Pittocks, Scotts, Ladds, and Greens. These were among the families he hoped the working class would replace in power. Boloff, a Russian immigrant, was a victim of Oregon's infamous Criminal Syndicalism Act under which he was sentenced to ten years in prison in 1930. He contracted tuberculosis, which his lawyer, IRVIN GOODMAN C20, attributed to medical neglect in the Oregon State Penitentiary. After two years of passionate pleas by his comrades, Boloff was released to the Multnomah County Poor Farm (now McMenamin's Edgefield Manor), when he was near death. The Party's leaflet for his mass funeral in the summer of 1932 says his last words echoed those of Frank Little, a Wobbly organizer who was lynched in Montana: "Tell the workers I fought for my class."[2]

4 The Portland Forum

The Portland Forum, established by Rabbi Stephen S. Wise and COLONEL C. E. S. WOOD B29 in 1905, provided lively public discussion of controversial subjects, including birth control and labor unions, along with scientific and medical topics. *The Oregonian* described it as:

> Like Hyde Park in London, this gathering comprises an intellectual melting pot which with its hurly-burly juxtaposition of good, bad and indifferent oratory reveal a vibrant cross section of viewpoints in all point of life as harbored by white collar business and office men, soft-shirted workers, grey-garbed professional men, ambitious politicians, fervid students—occasionally a housewife. Fully 99 per cent of the [450 member] Forum audience is made up of men who class themselves as philosophers, patriots, nationalists, socialists,

communists, technocrats and an occasional single taxer or non-partisanist.

After the new Central Public Library opened on **SW 10th Avenue between Taylor and Yamhill Streets**, it served as the organization's home until the Forum's demise during World War II.

Its two founders left Portland around 1920. Shortly after Wood moved to California, Wise resigned from the Portland Housing Code Advisory Committee, charging that it was "a front for realtors and homebuilders." He left the city to head New York's Central Synagogue. Tom Burns C19, one of the Forum's original members, became its informal "dean" through the late 1930s. In 1933, its permanent governing board included several members the Red Squad F26 identified as Communists, including civil engineer Richard Lovelace and student Kenneth Fitzgerald.

 Theodore "Ted" Jordan

Theodore "Ted" Jordan (1908–1969), a black railroad worker, was named Oregon's Scottsboro Case by the leftist ILD in 1932, when he was sentenced to death by hanging for killing a white man in the Klamath Falls railroad yards. Radicals mounted a successful campaign to save Jordan from execution, also led by Irvin Goodman C20 and the ILD, despite a bitter dispute over defense strategy with the Portland chapter of the local the National Association for the Advancement of Colored People (NAACP). In language that evokes the tenor of the times, Jordan wrote the following to promote the play *Pigment* by Portland radical Dawn Lovelace C16, produced by the ILD and the Save Jordan Anti-Lynch Committee, before several hundred people at the Italian Federation Hall F17 at **SW 4th Avenue and Madison Street**, on May Day 1934. *The Oregonian* thought it noteworthy that the play was "acted by Negroes and whites."

It is not an amusement, unless you can be amused by the sufferings, gropings, trusting and awakening of the 12 million Negro people and their ancestors for

generations back. It is not entertainment—unless the outcries of the Negro masses are entertaining. It is not tragedy—for there is nothing tragic about the uniting of the Negro and white millions, as they smash the barriers set up between them, and march, however painfully, toward a common liberation. It is drama—as only workers can feel it and express it. I urge every Negro worker—every white worker—to see it.
—Theodore Jordan
Death Cell, Oregon Penitentiary

Former Governor Julius L. Meier, citing racial prejudice, commuted his death sentence to life imprisonment in 1934 and Jordan served another twenty years in the penitentiary, where he took courses through the University of Oregon's extension division. According to *The Oregonian*, he became "a leading figure in convict life." Following an alleged deathbed confession by another man to the murder, Jordan was finally paroled from the Oregon State Penitentiary in 1954. But after winning a $500 settlement from Safeway in 1961 for a false accusation of shoplifting, he was convicted of a similar charge in 1963. He would go on to serve another two years in prison when the courts ordered a new trial on the original murder charge, which Klamath County declined to conduct. Jordan took courses at Reed College and was working as a janitor in a downtown building, living quietly in a NE Garfield Avenue bungalow and writing an autobiography when he died in 1969.

Jordan's lighthearted, teasing death cell correspondence with Belle Taub, who was sent to Portland by the ILD from New York to help organize Jordan's defense, was stolen by the Red Squad F26 in a "black bag job." Taken from the ILD office in room 307 of the McKay Building, his letter can be consulted in the Portland City Archive. A sample reads:

just took a small work-out on the piano here and goodness knows I am feeling like two million bucks even if it's in shekels or kopecks. Some day I may whip up a few hot numbers for you, provided you can stand it without calling the riot squad. Even if I do say so myself,

I seem to run Cab Calloway and Duke Ellington a very close second when it come to spanking the ivories, I plunk 'em mean or let 'em, alone—that's Mrs. George's [his mother's] boy as I live and breathe.

6 Elizabeth Gurley Flynn

Elizabeth Gurley Flynn (1890–1964), the Rebel Girl of Joe Hill's Wobbly song, lived with DR. MARIE D. EQUI B6 at her home at *1423 SW Hall Street* from 1926 to 1936. Both before and after those years, Flynn was a leader in national radical politics. As a pregnant young Wobbly, she was jailed overnight in Spokane during the IWW's free speech fights in 1909; as a sixty-four-year-old leader of the Communist Party during the McCarthy Era, she was imprisoned from 1955 to 1957 under the Smith Act. Her life in Portland was sedentary because of poor health. Flynn wrote: "I always felt I was in jail here." Despite her poor health, the 1934 LONGSHORE STRIKE C9 energized both her and Equi. Flynn recalled her anger that "workers' blood was shed." She and Equi contributed a joint article on the first anniversary of Portland's BLOODY WEDNESDAY C9 to the radical Seattle paper, *Voice of Action*. Later, as a Communist Party leader, Flynn visited Portland often, writing her observations about the political consequences of the VANPORT FLOOD D21, and speaking at a 1943 May Day Victory Rally in REDMEN HALL D25. Her first public lecture after her release from prison was in May 1958 at Reed College. She went to Moscow for medical treatment and died there in 1964. Some of her ashes were buried near JOHN REED'S B20. In 2002, a Wobbly entry in Portland's soapbox derby, E. G. Flynn, was named for her.

7 New Golden West Hotel

In the 1930s, *Harlemania*, a musical review, played nightly at the **New Golden West Hotel** at 345 NW Irving Street. The musical was also featured at a rally there for the Scottsboro Boys sponsored by the ILD.

The hotel was a center of black community life for the

first half of the twentieth century, when it welcomed black
railroad workers from nearby Union Station. From 1906
to 1931, it was managed by W. D. Allen. Mrs. Catherine
Byrd took over the job in 1933. Over the years, it housed
Richard Waldo Bogle's barber shop, a Chinese restaurant, a
saloon, an ice cream parlor, a candy store, and a speakeasy
during Prohibition—old timers recall having their first
drinks there, when a whiskey sour was a quarter.[3]

 8 Karl Marx Saltveit

Karl Marx Saltveit (1906–1978) was named in honor of
the German philosopher and economist by his Nor-
wegian Communist father. He anglicized his name to
"Carl" and put it on his barbershop at ***2946 NE Glisan
Street*** in the early 1930s. In 2006, the site was occupied
by what was claimed to be Portland's oldest body-
piercing salon. Saltveit named his own son, a former
Oregon Assistant Labor Commissioner, Carl Marcus,
who in turn, named the family's next first-born male
Carl Mark.

 9 1934 Maritime Strike & the International
Longshore and Warehouse Union (ILWU)

The outstanding Portland event of the 1930s was the
Maritime Strike of 1934. The event climaxed when
police shot and wounded four striking longshoremen
at St. Johns Terminal Four on July 11, the day referred
to as Bloody Wednesday. While not as notorious as
San Francisco's Bloody Thursday of July 5, 1934, when
police killed two workers, it was seen as a major battle
of Portland's class war. The shooting was instigated by
Mayor Joe Carson, who had tried to break the strike
by escorting scabs through picket lines and deputizing
Citizens Emergency Committee vigilantes as special
police. But on Bloody Wednesday he ordered regular
Portland police to escort a train onto the struck docks.
The police fired on the picket line assembled on the
railroad tracks in Pier Park wounding Burt Yates, E. W.
Beatty, W. Huntington, and Peter Stevenson.

At city hall, strike leader Matt Meehan confronted the mayor with the blood-soaked shirt of one of the wounded and yelled: "You're responsible for this!" After this incident the mayor was forever known in the labor community as Bloody Shirt Carson.

A week later, President Roosevelt sent New York Senator Robert Wagner to Terminal Four to smooth the waters, but Wagner's party was also fired upon. Although the incident was presumed a mistake, this time the fault was in the hands of the special police. The strike ended in victory for the longshoremen a few days later and led to the formation of today's **ILWU**. Several Oregon communities are home to locals of this union, including Locals 8 and 40 (Portland), 50 (Astoria), 17 (North Bend), 5 (Powell's Books) and the Columbia River Pensioners Association. Every year since 1934, on Bloody Thursday the ILWU commemorates the strike in every port on the Pacific Coast. For much of that time, Portland longshore-men marched through downtown to the sea wall, but now they meet at Oaks Park. According to veterans of the 1934 strike, Portlanders could still dig police bullets out of the big firs at Pier Park many years later.

10 Albina Hall

On August 20, 1934, **Albina Hall** at *1401 NE Alberta Street* was the scene of a violent shootout in one of the last bloody consequences of the great 1934 STRIKE C9. The hall was used to dispatch longshoremen belonging to a company union supported by the waterfront employ-ers, although the strike had officially ended in a famous union victory several weeks earlier. Longshoremen demonstrated outside the hall against company union workers on the docks and a one of them, James Con-nor, was shot and killed inside the hall. Police arrested twenty-nine ILA members on homicide charges and jailed them for about a month before the charges were dropped. The twenty-nine innocent men included for-mer Wobbly and radical strike leader William Pilcher,[4] as well as retired longshoreman Marvin Ricks, the last surviving Portland veteran of the 1934 strike. Ricks says

Connor was probably shot accidentally by his fellow scabs, who, led by the notorious RED SQUAD F26 provocateur Harper Knowles, fired at the union demonstrators from inside the hall.

 The Marine Workers Industrial Union

During the 1934 MARITIME STRIKE C9, **The Marine Workers Industrial Union**, a radical alternative to the American Federation of Labor's (AFL) corrupt ILA, had its headquarters in the former Foster Hotel Building at **NW 2nd Avenue and Davis Street**. As a union led by Communists, the Portland police raided it twice in July 1934, and its leaders were charged with violating the Oregon Criminal Syndicalism Act.

Nearby at **9 NW 3rd Avenue**, five women strike sympathizers working at the Villa Rooms—Margie, Kay, Florence, Helen, and "Smiles"—prepared sandwiches for the strikers (delivered by Broadway Cab drivers to the picket lines for free) and signed a card for them. It was rumored that they also provided strikers with other services on credit for the duration of the strike.

The ninety-plus striker to whom the women gave the card says "Smiles" was the working name of one of the five women. He added that to this day he always takes Broadway Cab cars because their drivers delivered those sandwiches to the picket lines for free.

 Admiral Evans

A major event in the 1934 MARITIME STRIKE C9 was the strikers' attack on the **Admiral Evans**, a scab hotel tied up at McCormick Dock just north of the Steel Bridge. Strikebreakers hired by the Citizens Emergency Committee were brought into Portland and housed aboard the ship. On May 11, as many as one hundred longshoremen formed what they called a riot squad; and after attacking armed guards, the group succeeded in boarding the vessel. The pitched battle ended with injured on both sides, but the longshoremen were victorious. Many of the special police had to swim for safety in

the Willamette River, as the *Evans* drifted downstream
until it wedged against the Broadway Bridge.

 13 The Union Hall

During the 1934 strike, and for many years after, the
union hall was at ***NW 8th Avenue and Everett Street***,
across from what was then French's Restaurant, where
the strikers used the phone to coordinate resistance by
topping strikebreakers' moves with roving "riot" and
picket squads. When longshoremen voted to organize
the CIO's ILWU in 1936, they retained the old building
as their hiring hall. After some years at ***NW 16th Avenue
and Glisan Street*** (now McMenamin's Mission Theater),
Local 8 built a new hall at ***NW Front Street and 21st
Avenue***, near Molly McGuires tavern, which was named
after the militant nineteenth century Irish miners' union
in the Pennsylvania coal fields.

 14 Lieutenant William Epps

Portland Police **Lieutenant William Epps** suffered a
black eye on the second day of the 1934 maritime strike,
when strikers prevented scabs from being bussed from
the Everett Street hall. But Lt. Epps, a former organizer
of the mineworkers' union, was evidently a working class
sympathizer. In 1932, he persuaded his superiors from
ordering an attack on an unemployed demonstration at
the Benson Hotel at ***309 SW Broadway***. Rumor has it
that later in the 1934 strike, Epps tipped off the strikers
about when and where police were escorting scabs.

Epps's son, David C. Epps, was a member of the OCF
C25, and American Friends of China C23 in the late 1930s.

 15 Dirk DeJonge

Communist leader **Dirk DeJonge** (1891–1976) was
imprisoned for almost two years, under Oregon's Criminal Syndicalism Act for chairing a meeting to protest
vigilante violence during the 1934 Maritime Strike C9. In
1935, the ILD produced a play, *The Trial of Dirk DeJonge*,

at the Woodmen of the World Hall at **SW 11th Avenue and Alder Street**. This play was part of a program where *Art Dancing* by attorney Nick Chaivoe was featured. DeJonge remains prominent in legal history in the case *DeJonge vs. Oregon*, where the U.S. Supreme Court ruled the Oregon law could not be used to convict a person for speech alone. DeJonge's "intended wife," Ella Badgley, wrote poignant but unsuccessful letters pleading his good character to the sentencing judge, Judge Jacob Kanzler, from her home at **23 N. Graham Street**. The letters found their way to the RED SQUAD F26 and can be consulted in its files in the city archives.

 16 Major Lawrence A. Milner & Dawn Lovelace

During the DeJonge trial at the Multnomah County Court House at **1021 SW 4th Avenue**, **Major Lawrence A. Milner** won applause from radicals when he revealed that special Oregon state prosecutor Stanley Doyle visited him at his home and offered to exchange his testimony against DeJonge for help on his government pension. However, Milner's declaration was an act to conceal that since 1933, he was a full-time paid undercover agent for Governor Charles "Iron Pants" Martin's National Guard.[5] While pretending to work for Left organizations through 1937, he wrote daily reports on leftist activities that today total about one thousand four hundred pages in the State Archives in Salem. When he came out as a witness against longshore union leader Harry Bridges in his deportation hearings, the deportation hearings chair recommended Milner "best be dismissed as a self-confessed liar."

Doyle was a notorious political extremist sponsored by the Commanders Council, which was comprised leaders of the American Legion and other right-wing and veterans groups. Portland radical **Dawn Lovelace** attacked him in her poem, *Stanley Doyle—Voice of Hunger, War and Fascism*, a stanza of which reads:

> He sneers-and from his mouth
> The Reichstag flames leap menacing and hot;

And all the outcries of the tortured minds and bodies
In fascist dungeons spring to vivid sound
And echo in the courtroom

 Thelma Johnson Streat

Thelma Johnson Streat (1912–1959) was a black
artist who grew up in Portland and graduated from
Washington High School in 1932. She lived at *1409 SE
Lambert Street* from 1934 to 1935 while she attended
the Museum Art School on a scholarship from PAUL
ROBESON D40. She then moved to San Francisco to work
as a WPA artist. The radical Mexican muralist Diego
Rivera, who owned some of Streat's work, considered it
"one of the most interesting manifestations of American
art...extremely evolved and sophisticated enough to
reconquer the grace and purity of African and American
art." Her paintings were also purchased by the Museum
of Modern Art in New York City, and by Hollywood
celebrities. Although she left Portland for California
in 1936, Streat later made visits to Portland as a dancer.
Reed College holds her painting, *Black Virgin*, in its
permanent collection.

 Dr. DeNorval Unthank

The prominent black physician **Dr. DeNorval Unthank**
was a special target of MAJOR LAWRENCE A. MILNER C16. When
Unthank arrived in Portland in 1930 to practice medicine, he and his wife were forced to move five times for
reasons that included being harassed from the Ladd's
Addition neighborhood. On August 20, 1935, Milner
accompanied Esther Murphy, wife of Communist leader
James Murphy, to meet Unthank in his offices at *SW
6th Avenue and Burnside Street* to discuss a meeting
on the Italian invasion of Ethiopia to be held at what
was then called the Colored Elks Temple. Unthank
offered to contact black churches and the YMCA to
promote the meeting and said his wife had just returned
from Ethiopia and would speak. Milner's report to the
Oregon National Guard concludes: "Unthank is a party

sympathizer, as he has various literature in his office and from his statements he is very anxious to promote any work that is sponsored by the party." A few days later, Milner observed Ken Fitzgerald, a Portland reporter for the Seattle labor paper, *Voice of Action*, interview Unthank about the racist obstacles he faced practicing his profession in Portland.

The only Portland park named for a "Communist Party sympathizer" is Unthank Park on **N. Commercial Avenue between N. Failing and Shaver Streets**.

19 Tom Burns

Tom Burns's (1876–1957) famous Clock Shop was located at **221 W. Burnside Street** since before World War I until the late 1950s. Burns was the son of a British Labor Party member of Parliament from Liverpool who came to Portland in 1905. Burns originally joined the Socialist Party but soon joined the IWW and opened his shop. Known both as "the mayor of Burnside," and "the most arrested man in Portland's history,"[6] Burns maintained a radical lending library in the basement and published *FAX*, an irreverent newsletter that attacked the Right as well as the Left.

During the 1930s, Burns frequently denounced "Portland's political parasites—the first families like the Corbetts, Labbes, Wilcoxes—coupon clipping clowns that never did a useful day's work in their worthless lives." Howard Morgan, a leader of the Oregon Democratic Party in the 1950s and 1960s, credits Burns as an important influence in his decision to enter politics.[7] The radical tradition of that Burnside intersection continued until just a few years ago. In 1996, the storefront next to Burns's former store was unwittingly occupied by an anarchist group, some of whom had ties to a resurrected IWW organization, and in 2001, a neighboring building was the site of an anarchist "Center for Revolution." Until a few days before he died, Burns used streetcars or buses to get to his shop from his home at **5913 SE 49th Avenue** just off Woodstock Boulevard, which is now a vacant lot.

 Irvin Goodman

Portland's most celebrated radical attorney, **Irvin Goodman** (1897–1958), rose to prominence in the 1930s. In 1940, he shared his office with Leo Levinson in suite 1002 of the Spaulding Building, having previously shared it with the future Federal Judge Gus Solomon. Goodman, a 1921 Reed College graduate, played a leading role in most of the important defenses of radicals and minorities in Portland throughout his professional life, including the famous DeJonge vs. Oregon Supreme Court Decision C15. Goodman was especially active in civil rights, defending such prominent victims of racism as Theodore "Ted" Jordan C5 and Wardell Henderson D19. Also among his clients were many victims of McCarthyism, including Soviet naval officer Lt. Nicholai Redin D8 and defiant witnesses at the 1954 House Un-American Activities Committee (HUAC) D32 hearings in Portland. Honored by the American Veterans Committee, the Oregon Committee for Protection of the Foreign Born D43, and the ILWU C9, he is buried in the Kesser Israel cemetery at **SE 67th Avenue and Nehalem Street**.

C: 1930s
Unions & Commies

 Grace Wicks

Grace Wicks was an activist and actress whose politics were a strange mixture of liberalism and far-right reaction. She moved to Portland from Salem in the mid-1920s after losing a struggle to prevent the hanging of Barney Cody, a cousin of Buffalo Bill who was tried for murder. Originally a supporter of FDR, she managed to include herself in the President's party when he dedicated Bonneville Dam in 1934. She became disillusioned when the New Deal failed to end the Great Depression and turned her support to the Ku Klux Klan, America First, and anti-Semitic groups. Her famous march up Broadway in 1935 marked her break to the left when one of the slogans on her barrel read "Wake Up Unemployed. Organize Now!" She ran for local and state office in the late 1930s and 1940s as a right-wing activist. Her future partner, Fred Melanson, wrote a campaign poem for her that included the line "To Oregon a Goddess came, who fights for the oppressed."[8]

 Burl (B. A.) Green

The courageous Portland attorney **Burl (B. A.) Green** often represented labor unions, especially during the 1930s. He tried to organize an Oregon chapter of the AMERICAN CIVIL LIBERTIES UNION (ACLU) D28, and chaired a December 1937 meeting at the Multnomah County Courthouse that exposed the illegal operation of the Police RED SQUAD F26. For his efforts, the Red Squad listed him as an "active Communist sympathizer." His record also includes defending Wobblies arrested in Tillamook while maintaining friendly personal relations with prominent Portlanders.

 Protesting Fascism

Portland radicals, led by the Communist Party, tried to warn Oregonians about the threat of fascism. One of their efforts was to protest the arrival of fascist ships, as in January 1936, when police arrested eleven Portlanders[9] demonstrating against the **Nazi cruiser *Emden*** docked at the foot of **SW Couch Street**. As *The Oregonian* described it, the *Emden*'s symbol was "The 'new deal' flag of Germany, the swastika, emblem of Hitler, unfurled to the breezes of Portland." The ship's officers visited Mayor Joseph Carson in his office, where "they clicked their heels in military fashion and gave him the German [Heil Hitler] salute." Most German organizations in Portland arranged welcoming entertainment for the crew. Until 1936, the *Emden* was commanded by future Grand Admiral Karl Doenitz who, as Hitler's successor, formally surrendered Nazi Germany in 1945. In addition to the demonstration at the seawall, the Portland section of the Communist Party called on unions and Jewish organizations to send protest delegations to the mayor and urged maritime unions to strike when the *Emden* docked.

The previous October, during the fascist invasion of Ethiopia, the Communist Party organized a significant picket line at the Clark-Wilson and Oceanic Terminal to protest the docking of the Italian cargo ship the *S.S. Cellini*, asking longshoremen to "Load No Cargo for Fascist Italy" and to, "Turn around Mussolini's Ship of Death." Also in 1935, the Portland branch of the American League Against War and Fascism picketed the office of Robert Closetermann, the German consul in the Stock Exchange Building, declaring, "We Want No Fascism Here!" In 1938, protests by the **American Friends of China** (which, ironically, had its office in room 507 of the same building), and OWA C24, supported by Willamette Lodge 63 of the International Association of Machinists, targeted the Japanese training ship *Taisei Maru*. This ship docked at the foot of SW Ankeny Street for several days, and was welcomed by the Chamber of Commerce. At least fifteen people, including MARTINA GANGLE CURL F13, were arrested. Gus Karju, whose sailboat towed a float demanding "Stop Killing the Chinese" and "Japanese not welcome," was charged with "obstructing the river."

24 Oregon Workers Alliance

The 1936 Rose Festival parade featured an **OWA** float with MARTINA GANGLE CURL F13 as the Statue of Liberty. The association developed from the unemployed councils organized by the Oregon Communist Party early in the Great Depression. The councils demanded public relief and public works programs, and offered social activities such as the Hawthorne branch's "Chicken dinner, plenty of coffee, entertainment and dancing—all for 25 cents," at REDMEN HALL D25, *1510 SE 9th Avenue* at Hawthorne Boulevard. After several mergers with similar groups, the OWA emerged and described itself in Wobbly terms as the one big union of the unemployed, part-time workers, and workers on WPA and other relief projects. In addition to its original goals, the OWA was active in supporting families who were rejected for public welfare and were resisting evictions and utility cutoffs. During the McCarthy Era, some of its foreign-born working class members were deported or threatened with deportation. The OWA was organized into neighborhood locals, such as Abernethy Local No. 23, which met in the Abernethy School auditorium, then at **SE 14th Avenue at Division**. Its state office was in the GOVERNOR BUILDING C35 at 408 SW 2nd Avenue.

25 Oregon Commonwealth Federation & Monroe Sweetland

The **OCF**, a liberal and radical coalition of New Deal supporters founded in 1936 with a local electoral agenda, had its offices in the Stock Exchange Building at **170 SW 3rd Avenue.** Under the leadership of the late **Monroe Sweetland** (1910–2006), who later became a prominent Democrat, the OCF backed several successful campaigns for the state legislature and local government. Like many coalitions of the 1930s, the OCF suffered from disputes among its component organizations. Ben Osborne, secretary of the Oregon Federation of Labor, considered the OCF to be "influenced by the Communist Party" and a "back door to the CIO," which was the AFL's new industrial union challenger. On the other hand, the OREGON SOCIALIST PARTY B28 withdrew from the OCF in 1938 because the socialists charged it had become an appendage to the Democratic Party and made deals with capitalist politicians.

 Harry Gross

Radical attorney **Harry Gross** (1902–1938) was active in the OCF C25, representing CIO labor organizers and other radicals until his sudden death from a heart attack at a young age. At his funeral, former Governor Oswald West noted that Gross "would have been a wealthy man if he had chosen to serve Mannon instead of the poor and oppressed." Three judges as well as future Federal Judge Gus Solomon and two city commissioners (Ralph Clyde and Jake Bennett) were among the honorary pallbearers at his funeral.

27 The Abraham Lincoln Brigade

At least eleven Oregon volunteers joined the
Abraham Lincoln Brigade to defend the Spanish
Republic against a fascist invasion backed by Hitler and
Mussolini between 1936 and 1939. One who gave his
life to fight fascism was William Newton Miller, who
grew up on a farm near Dayton, Oregon, and joined
the Communist Party in Portland. Miller was killed at
age twenty-five in one of the last battles of the Lincoln
Brigade. Before going to Spain, he was the roommate
of Harry Wayland Randall, another Lincoln Brigade
member and a 1937 Reed College graduate. Carl Lee
Bellows, a Klamath Falls CIO union organizer, and
Martin David "Toivo" Maki, originally from Astoria,
were both wounded while fighting in the Brigade.
Other Oregonians who went to Spain were Virgil Lanny
Morris (a seaman and member of the National Maritime
Union), Thomas Allen Norton (a poet, writer, and a
Reed College student), Len Fletcher Spencer (also of
Klamath Falls), Harold Spring (a young Communist who
died while fighting fascism in Italy with the U.S. Army
in World War II), and Carl Ralph Syvanen (of Astoria).
Earl Clyde Steward of Irrigon in Morrow County also
fought with the Abraham Lincoln Brigade, and he, along
with the others, was later called a premature anti-fascist.
On his return from Spain, Steward lived at **3435 NE 79th
Avenue**.

Captain Harry Johnson, a Portland ship captain,
commanded several relief ships to Spain and personally
presented a document signed by Helen Keller, Theodore
Dreiser, and one thousand others pledging their commitment to Republican Spain.

In 2007, the only surviving veteran of the Lincoln
Brigade living in Portland was Virginia Malbin, who
went to Spain with her late husband, Dr. Bernard
Malbin. She worked in Barcelona assisting members
of the international brigades and had firearms training.
The couple later moved to Oregon where Dr. Malbin
joined KAISER PERMANENTE D23. Portlanders raised money
to send an ambulance to the Spanish government and

on February 28, 1937, three thousand people filled the Portland Civic Auditorium at *222 SW Clay Street*, now Keller Auditorium, to honor representatives of the Spanish Republic.

 **Bert Cantor**

In 1937, Lincoln High School student **Bert Cantor** was interrogated by a member of the Portland Police RED SQUAD F26 about his leadership of his school's chapter of the American Student Union (ASU). This chapter met in room 428 of the high school (now Lincoln Hall of Portland State University, *1200 SW Park Avenue*). The Red Squad officer was ordered to question Cantor by right-wing Portland school board member Louis Starr. Starr had declared that the ASU was a Communist organization and should be barred from Portland schools. The Squad officer accused Cantor of being a member of the Young Communist League and gave him a pamphlet entitled *Americanism or Communism?* But another school board member and 1924 Reed graduate, Harry Kenin, was outraged by Starr's link to the Red Squad and his attempt to intimidate Cantor, as was Lincoln principal Henry Gunn, who believed there was nothing wrong with the club. Cantor later joined labor attorney BURL (B. A.) GREEN C22, head of an early Oregon chapter of the ACLU D28, and other speakers to denounce the Red Squad at an ACLU meeting in the County Courthouse.

 Valery Chkalov

Off the Lewis and Clark Highway at the Pearson Airpark, *1115 E. 5th Street in Vancouver, Washington*, is the only monument to heroes of the former Soviet Union in the United States. The monument commemorates the over-the-Pole flight of **Valery Chkalov** (for whom a street in Vancouver is named), Georgii Baidukov, and Alexander Belyakov. These men were the three Soviet fliers who flew over the North Pole in an Antonov-25 and landed in Vancouver on June 20, 1937. General George Marshall was commander of the

Vancouver Barracks at the time, and his widow recalled that he asked Aaron Frank to send clothes for the flyers, who only had huge fur parkas when they landed. A Moscow-to-Vancouver committee tried and failed to raise funds for a monument in 1937, but one was finally erected in 1975. Portland businessman Alan Cole was awarded the Order of Friendship by Russian President Boris Yeltsin in 1996 for leading the private effort to erect the monument.

 30 Minor White

The renowned photographer **Minor White** lived on quaint **SW Cable Street** and at the old YMCA building when he photographed Portland scenes for the WPA in 1940. In 1938, he also was politically active as acting secretary of the Peoples' Power League of Oregon, a militant public power advocacy group that met in room 302 of the Oregon Building downtown. White also worked at the WPA Art Center in La Grande.

31 Oregon Federal Theater

The WPA's **Oregon Federal Theater** produced radical plays such as *One Third of a Nation* in 1938 at the former Elks' Club, **914 SW 10th Avenue**, now part of the Governor Hotel, where the CITY CLUB OF PORTLAND F3 meets.

 32 Dorothea Lange, Arthur Rothstein & Bill Lee

The prominent Farm Security Administration photographers **Dorothea Lange, Arthur Rothstein, and Bill Lee** all documented Portland scenes, including Hoovervilles, traveling all over the state to produce a compelling portrait of late 1930s Oregon. Although over a thousand of the images are available at the Library of Congress, no comprehensive exhibit of that collection has been presented anywhere in the state.

 **33** Ray Becker

Ray Becker (1900–1950) was the last of the nine WOBBLIES B7 imprisoned in the wake of the 1919 CENTRALIA MASSACRE B27. From a "preacher family," he intended to become a "sky pilot" but joined the IWW instead. As the radical writer Anna Louise Strong's poem about Becker goes:

> But I figure
> The only practical Christians
> TODAY
> Are the I.W.W.'s
> And the Socialists
> And the folks
> That are trying to get
> A NEW WORLD!

Becker arrived in Portland after his sentence was commuted in 1939. Unlike his comrades, and despite the advice of his attorney IRVIN GOODMAN C20, Becker refused an earlier-offered parole because he maintained his innocence. A large crowd of supporters greeted Becker at Union Station when he was finally freed in 1939, and he was welcomed at CIO headquarters in the GOVERNOR BUILDING C35. A reception was planned at a Portland restaurant but, when organizers learned the restaurant refused to serve blacks, the event was moved to the Bohemian, then at *910 SW Washington Street*. JULIA EATON RUUTTILA F10 was Becker's close friend, and she became secretary of the Free Ray Becker Committee, established in 1936 by the CIO's International Woodworkers of America (IWA) union, whose Klamath Falls Local made Becker an honorary member. For publicity photos, Ruuttila wore a bracelet fashioned by Becker. After his release, Becker ran a small craft shop in Vancouver and lived in a cabin south of Portland until his death in 1950. At his funeral, Ruuttila put a red rose in his lapel—a tradition for old Wobblies.

C: 1930s
Unions & Commies

Jessie M. Short

Jessie M. Short was a member of the Portland school board from 1934 to 1937, the Federal Arts Committee and the city's Housing Code Committee for twenty years. She was also a professor of mathematics at Reed College until she retired in 1939. For focusing public attention on primitive housing conditions that maintained fat slumlord profits, as well as support of numerous progressive causes, the Police Red Squad F26 called her a "Communist and dangerous radical."

 The Governor Building

In the 1930s the **Governor Building** at *408 SW 2nd Avenue* hosted the offices of many working-class organizations. These included the state CIO and its newspaper, *Labor New Dealer* (room 314), the IWA (room 418), the dispatch office of the Marine Cooks & Stewards branch, the local chapter of the Harry Bridges Defense Committee (room 315 in 1939), the OWA C24, the Civic Emergency Federation, and the Portland May Day 1939 Action Committee (room 324.) The Governor also had housed the local Ku Klux Klan during the group's heyday in the 1920s.

 Commissioner Ralph C. Clyde

One of the most outspoken proponents of a Peoples Utility District in the 1930s was **Portland City Commissioner Ralph C. Clyde**, often re-elected for his populist political outlook. He was first elected in 1931 and remained a council member until he died in 1943. He fought private utilities, supported labor unions, and his efforts were remembered in later attempts to reform Portland General Electric into a public utility.

 The Golden Pheasant

The Golden Pheasant restaurant, located on *SW 4th Avenue between Alder and Washington Streets*, was a favorite gathering place for liberal and radical Port-landers in the late 1930s. These radicals included the Oregon Friends of China, the Progressive Municipal Political Club and the OCF c25. The federation's executive secretary MONROE SWEETLAND c25 (later a leader of the Democratic Party in Oregon) recalled that in the late 1930s, its poorly paid staff was often fed with a large bowl of noodles at The Golden Pheasant, courtesy of attorney Gus Solomon, one of the few in the political group with a steady income.

1930s Notes

1. Paul Dickson and Thomas B. Allen, *The Bonus Army: An American Epic* (New York: Walker and Company, 2005).

2. John Terry, *The Oregonian*, April 16, 2006.

3. Bunny Doar, interview. Gearhart, Oregon (1998).

4. The late Dr. William "Billy" Pilcher, Harry's son, returned to the Portland waterfront after an academic career as an anthropology professor. His doctoral thesis was published as *The Portland Longshoremen: A Dispersed Urban Community* (New York: Holt, Rinehart, and Winston, 1972).

5. Gary Murrell, *Iron Pants: Oregon Anti-New Deal Governor, Charles Henry Martin* (Seattle: Washington State University Press, 2000).

6. *The Oregonian*, October 18, 1931.

7. Craig Wollner and W. Tracy Dillon (Eds). "Recollections of Tom Burns" *A Richer Harvest: The Literature of Work in the Pacific Northwest* (Corvallis, OR: Oregon State University Press, 1999).

8. June M. Benowitz, *Days of Discontent: American Women and Right-Wing Politics, 1933–1945*, (DeKalb, IL: Northern Illinois University Press, 2002), 54–79.

9. They included future Lincoln Brigade vet Earl Steward, Esther Layton, secretary of the Portland League Against War and Fascism, Violet Olsen, Lillian Foster, Frank Webber, Lavena Bennett, Mary Gould, Seth Nordling, and Reed students John Hammond, Robert Lewis, and William Hood.

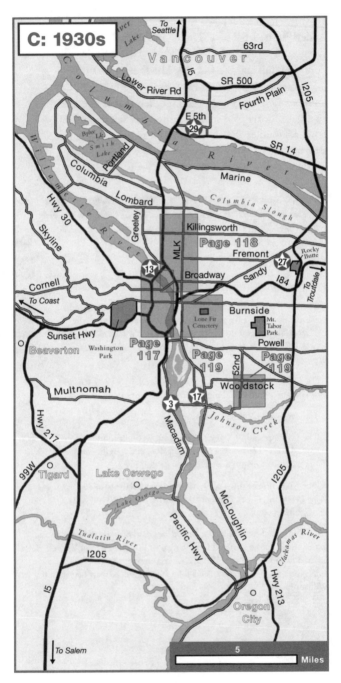

C: 1930s

To Seattle

Vancouver

63rd

Lower River Rd

SR 500

Fourth Plain

I5

I205

E 5th

29

SR 14

Columbia River

Marine

Bybee Lk.

Smith Lake

Portland

Columbia

Lombard

Columbia Slough

Hwy 30

Greeley

Killingsworth

Page 118

Fremont

Skyline

MLK

Rocky Butte

13

Broadway

Sandy

27

Cornell

I84

To Troutdale

To Coast

Burnside

Sunset Hwy

Lone Fir Cemetery

Mt. Tabor Park

Beaverton

Washington Park

Page 117

Powell

Multnomah

Page 119

Page 119

52nd

Woodstock

Hwy 217

3

17

Johnson Creek

Macadam

99W

Tigard

Lake Oswego

Lake Oswego

McLoughlin

I205

Pacific Hwy

Tualatin River

I205

Clackamas River

Hwy 213

I5

Oregon City

To Salem

5

Miles

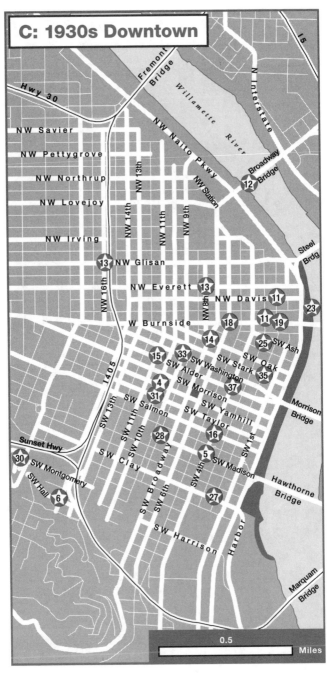

C: 1930s Downtown

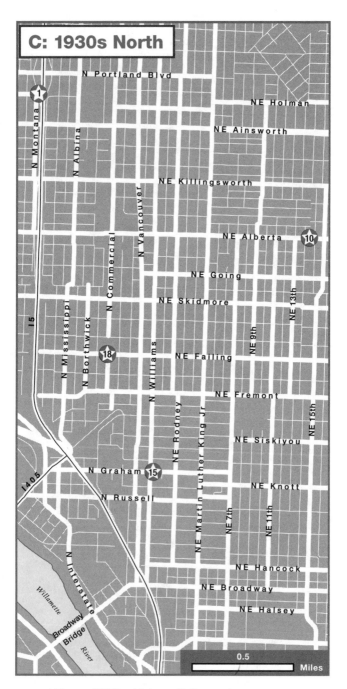

C: 1930s North

N Portland Blvd

NE Holman

NE Ainsworth

N Montana

N Albina

NE Killingsworth

N Vancouver

NE Alberta

NE Going

NE Skidmore

N Commercial

NE 13th

I 5

N Mississippi

N Borthwick

NE Failing

NE 9th

N Williams

NE Fremont

NE Rodney

NE 15th

NE Siskiyou

I 405

N Graham

NE Knott

N Russell

NE Martin Luther King Jr

NE 7th

NE 11th

N Interstate

NE Hancock

Willamette

NE Broadway

Broadway
Bridge

NE Halsey

River

0.5

Miles

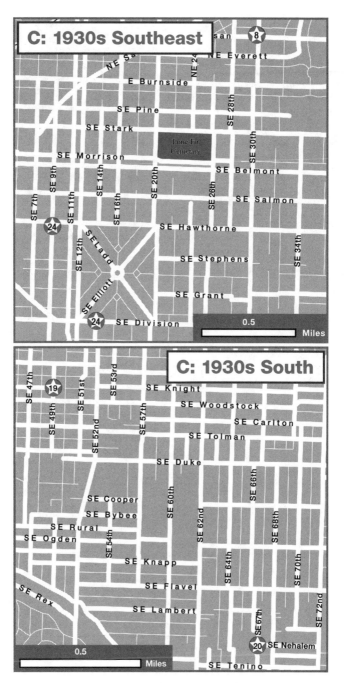

C: 1930s Southeast

NE Sandy
NE Everett
E Burnside
SE Pine
SE Stark
SE Morrison
SE Belmont
SE Salmon
SE Hawthorne
SE Stephens
SE Grant
SE Division

Lone Fir Cemetery

SE 7th
SE 9th
SE 11th
SE 12th
SE Ladd
SE 14th
SE 16th
SE Elliott
SE 20th
SE 26th
SE 28th
SE 30th
SE 34th
NE 24th

0.5 Miles

C: 1930s South

SE Knight
SE Woodstock
SE Carlton
SE Tolman
SE Duke
SE Cooper
SE Bybee
SE Rural
SE Ogden
SE Knapp
SE Flavel
SE Rex
SE Lambert
SE Nehalem
SE Tenino

SE 47th
SE 49th
SE 51st
SE 52nd
SE 53rd
SE 54th
SE 57th
SE 60th
SE 62nd
SE 64th
SE 66th
SE 67th
SE 68th
SE 70th
SE 72nd

0.5 Miles

This August 1932 protest in Lownsdale Square A7 was billed as an antiwar rally. There were also signs demanding veterans be paid their bonus and for the release of labor leader Tom Mooney. *City of Portland Archives, A2001-74.91.*

VETERANS MARCH!

BE IN WASHINGTON--MAY-12-1933

Attention M E N !

YOU, the "Forgotten People" (Veterans, Farmers, and Workers), have petitioned Congress!

YOU have written letters to your Congressmen and Senators!

YOU have had your friends, and neighbors do the same!

YOU have removed from office the Hoover administration and those who opposed your just demands!

N O W --

You must march! March to your National Capital to save your country from those who continue to pillage it and deny you your just demands under a new administration.

The nation is at the crossroads: the road to fascism and despotism and the road to democracy and freedom. Behind the greatest flood of propaganda ever let loose upon a suffering nation, your enemies are fast setting at naught all the gains you made and penalizing the veterans, the unemployed and farmers.

Thousands of your disabled comrades are about to be thrown onto the streets and highways of the country. Hundreds of thousands are having their meagre allowances taken away. Hospital and domiciliary care will be denied them. Spanish-American and Civil War veterans, despite their advanced years, find their only security against old age wiped away. The same onslaught cuts the wages of the humble government employee to the bone.

It is an attack, a direct attack upon the American standard of living, a policy that calls for labor camps for the unemployed, dictators for the farmers and penury for the veterans. There can be but one answer to this brutal attack:

V. E. L. C. Bulletin No. 5.

This Bonus March flier exhorted veterans to "March to your National Capital to save your country from those who continue to pillage it and deny you your just demands under a new administration." *City of Portland Archives, A2001-074.b2.f9.*

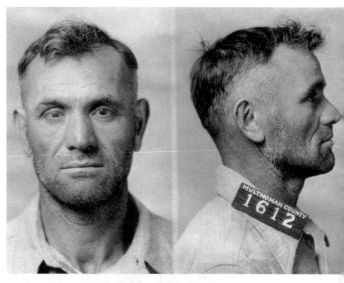

 Ben Boloff's mug shot upon his arrest on November 1, 1930. He was tried and convicted under Oregon's Criminal Syndicalism Act, and spent ten years in prison. *City of Portland Archives, A2001-074.*

 This flier announced the demonstration and mass funeral procession for Ben Boloff, who died from tuberculosis shortly after being released from prison. *City of Portland Archives, A2001-074.*

8

The Carl Marx Barber Shop was located at 2946 NE Glisan Street in the early 1930s. *Carl Saltveit.*

FRAMED –
NOT GUILTY

Mass Protest Meeting

THURSDAY,
Sept. 14, 8 p. m.

Colored Elks Hall
1712 Williams Ave.
Corner Cherry

NEGRO AND WHITE
COME IN MASS

Admission Free

JORDAN
MUST NOT HANG!

Speakers

DR. VIRGIL McMICKLE
Champion of the Oppressed

ROBT. CREAMER
Prominent Portland Attorney

JAMES MURPHY
National Lumber Workers' Union

HARRY JACKSON
of New York
Marine Workers' Industrial Union

WILLIAM SIDNEY
Oregon Section International Labor Defense

OREGON STATE SUPREME COURT, Salem, Oregon:

THEODORE JORDAN, young Negro worker, now under death sentence in the Oregon State Penitentiary, was framed on purely circumstantial evidence and on "confessions" forced from him under the most brutal and inhuman third-degree torture.

❦ Jordan was framed because he is a Negro, because he was an unemployed worker and because of a previous prison record.

❦ We, therefore demand that the Oregon State Supreme Court reverse the verdict of the Klamath Falls Court and that the innocent Theodore Jordan be immediately and unconditionally released.

Signed_____

5

Advertisements like this were seen all over Portland protesting the death sentence for Ted Jordan. This flier has a statement designed to send to the Oregon Supreme Court, demanding that the Court reverse the verdict of the Klamath Falls Court. *City of Portland Archives, A2001-074.*

 Richard Correll's labor woodcuts began appearing in the Seattle paper *Voice of Action* in the 1930s. This one, titled *Bloody Wednesday at Terminal 4* appeared on the one-year anniversary of that date in 1935. *Michael Munk.*

 Portland Police escorted "scabs" through picket lines outside a hiring hall, a building used by companies to hire workers. *Oregon Historical Society, OrHi81704.*

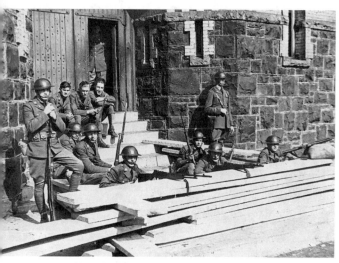

 The Oregon National Guard was called in to man the barricade against strikers at the Multnomah County Armory at NW 10th Avenue and Couch Street. *Oregon Historical Society, CN005984.*

 In August 1934, twenty-nine innocent ILA men were arrested and jailed for a month on homicide charges. Marvin Ricks (left), the last surviving Portland veteran of the 1934 Strike, was one of those innocent men. This pin (inset) was worn by their supporters. *Michael Munk.*

 13 The Union Hall was once located in what is now McMenamin's Mission Theater at NW 16th Avenue and Glisan Street. *Colin Smith.*

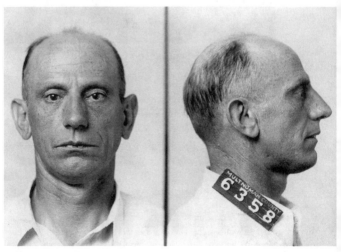

 15 Communist leader Dirk DeJonge was imprisoned for nearly two years for chairing a meeting protesting vigilante violence during the 1934 strike. His mug shot was taken on July 18, 1934. *City of Portland Archives, A2001-74.*

 Tom Burns's bookstore, the famous Clock Shop, was located at 221 W. Burnside Street. He was a member of both the Socialist Party and then the IWW. Burns was known both as "the mayor of Burnside," and "the most arrested man in Portland's history." He had a radical lending library in the basement of Clock Shop and published *FAX*, and irreverent newsletter attacking both the Right and the Left. *Walt Curtis.*

 Top: The interior of The Clock Shop. *Walt Curtis.*
Bottom: The Clock Shop became the United Clothing Co. Union
Store, and later the Liberation Collective, as pictured above in 2004.
Michael Munk.

 Dr. DeNorval Unthank is the only "Communist Party sympathizer" to have a Portland park named for him. Unthank Park is located on N. Commercial Avenue. *Oregon Historical Society, OrHi25442.*

 Grace Wicks, an activist and actress, had a strange mix of liberalism and far-right reaction in her politics. She's shown here, in 1935, during a political march in Portland. *Oregon Historical Society, CN023435.*

Portland's radicals protested the United States's support of Japan in its war with China. The Women's Committee of the American League for Peace and Democracy are shown at the waterfront in 1937. *City of Portland Archives, A2001-074.23.*

The German ship *Emden* was enthusiastically welcomed by Portland's powerful in 1936. Radicals protested it. *Historical Photo Archive, Monner 2271.*

 The Oregon Workers Alliance float in the 1937 Rose Festival Parade featured Martina Gangle Curl F13 as Liberty. *Hank Curl.*

 Harry Gross was a radical attorney in Portland until his death at the age of thirty-six in 1938. This picture was taken March 14, 1932, and kept by the Red Squad F26. *City of Portland Archives, A2001-074.17.*

 Arthur Rothstein took this photograph of a man living in a Portland Hooverville during the Depression, July 1936. *Library of Congress, LC-USF34-004817-E.*

 This flier called Americans to support the Spanish fight against fascism and to hear Spaniards speak in May of 1938. *City of Portland Archives, A2001-074.*

 On May 29, 1941, the Harry Bridges Defense Committee held a benefit dinner at the Governor Building. Morris H. Goodman, Mrs. MacGregor, and Mr. Rodman were identified and photographed by the Red Squad F26. *City of Portland Archives, A2001-074.83.*

 The Governor Building hosted the offices of many working-class organizations during the 1930s. They included the state CIO and its newspaper, the IWA, the OWA C24, and the Portland May Day 1939 Action Committee. On the other end of the spectrum, the building had hosted the Ku Klux Klan in the 1920s. *Colin Smith.*

Members of the International Longshore and Warehouse Union (ILWU) on the Portland picket lines during the 1948 Pacific Coast longshore strike. Don Wollam, one of the Portland Four, is on the far left, and Jesse Stranahan is standing next to him. *ILWU Archives.*

D: World War II–1960
McCarthyism & Cold War

> Portland is OK except for being fifty years behind Seattle
> in radical temper…
> —Woody Guthrie, 1947[1]

When Nazi Germany invaded the Soviet Union seven
months before Pearl Harbor, the Communist Left
quickly shifted from opposition to U.S. participation in
the European war into enthusiastic support for military
action against fascism that lasted for the duration of
World War II. Even after having sent about a dozen
Oregonians—its "premature" anti-fascists—TO FIGHT IN SPAIN
DURING THE LATE 1930S C27, until June 1941, the Communist
Party was among many groups warning Americans
against entering another imperialist war like World War I.

Thousands of Japanese American Oregonians were
herded behind barbed wire at the PACIFIC INTERNATIONAL LIVE-
STOCK EXPOSITION BUILDING D5 following U.S. entry into the war.
After being confined for the summer of 1942's sweltering
months in the exposition building's foul-smelling animal
stalls, they were shipped off—mainly to a concentration camp at Minidoka, Idaho. In 2006, Gresham was
embarrassed when a memorial to its wartime mayor was
cancelled when he was revealed as a racist who opposed
the return of local citizens deported to concentration
camps. He was not alone. A survey of businesses by the
Portland Chamber of Commerce showed only two of
one hundred and twenty-five answered "yes" to the
question: "Should loyal Japanese be permitted to return
to Pacific coast states during the war?"[2]

The wartime shipyards Henry Kaiser built in Portland
and Vancouver transformed the city both economi-
cally and socially. But when thousands of black workers
arrived in Portland they were segregated into a Jim

Crow "auxiliary" by Tommy Ray, head of the all-white BOILERMAKERS UNION LOCAL 72 D10. And all Portland black people faced tightened restrictions on housing and notorious "white trade only" signs on numerous retail and restaurant businesses. Some leftists worried that protests against such discrimination might divert their energy from the war effort.

Portland also became a major port for shipping lend-lease supplies to back the Soviet war effort, which was evidently a popular cause in the city. A November 8, 1941, *Oregon Journal* editorial over-enthusiastically celebrated the Bolshevik Revolution by describing a statue to John Reed that doesn't exist:

> Today, one of our great allies, the Union of Soviet Socialist Republics, celebrates the 25th anniversary of its founding. November 8, 1917, was the final day of the "10 days that shook the world," as they were named by Jack Reed of Portland, Oregon, whose statute stands in Red Square in Moscow and who is honored by the Russians as we honor great Europeans who helped America in its war for freedom.

The editorial concludes in boldface type:

> We of the U.S. can pause today to extend hands across the Bering Sea to a friend that has never failed to stand beside American democracy…

Communist Party activities in Portland during World War II emphasized the role of women in the war effort and as Communist political leaders. In 1942, the Multnomah County Communist Party held a "Daughters of America" birthday celebration for national party leaders Ella Reeve "Mother" Bloor (75) and Anita Whitney (80) at 721 SW 11th Avenue. They called for attacks against German defenses in Western Europe as a "second front" to help the Soviet Union's struggle in the East. ELIZABETH GURLEY FLYNN C6 spoke to a May Day Victory Rally in 1943 sponsored by the Multnomah County Communist Party at REDMEN HALL D25, which then was the state party headquarters. A few months later, in July, Communist Party National Chair WILLIAM Z. FOSTER B1, speaking at a public meeting before two hundred and fifty people at Benson High School, urged labor unions to forgo their right to strike rule for the duration. American Youth for Democracy called upon young women to join "Sweethearts of Servicemen" (SOS), which proposed: "Let's get acquainted with other SOSers, to have parties and teas, knit or sew, go bowling and hiking, and do a little bit more to help win the war and bring him back sooner."

After the war, Flynn returned for May Day 1946, speaking against "the menace of World War III" at the Shattuck School on Broadway (now part of the Portland State University campus). For May Day 1948, Trinidad native Claudia Jones, secretary of the Communist Party's Women's Commission, spoke at Norse Hall F17. Jones was an important spokesperson for black and women's rights—as well as a relentless critic of male chauvinism. In 1951 she was imprisoned together with Flynn and other national party leaders for "advocating the violent overthrow of the U.S. government" under the infamous Smith Act and later deported to England.

With victory in the war, the Left and labor coalitions that had supported the New Deal expected that its record of militant wartime patriotism would help gain it mass support in the political arena. But as a Cold War between the United States and the Soviet Union quickly became the dominant narrative of the postwar years, the American Communists' wartime ties to the "heroic" Soviet Union became a liability. The entire Left and labor coalition came under media suspicion as disloyal and subversive and became a target of massive government suppression.

The Old Left's final major effort was the originally hopeful Progressive Party D25 campaign of 1948, which was led by former vice president Henry Wallace. But he drew only three percent of the vote in Oregon (the Socialist Party received about one percent). An even greater blow to the nation's Left was delivered in Portland a few months later, when the Congress of Industrial Organizations (CIO) tenth national convention met in Portland's Masonic Temple (today the Mark Building of the Portland Art Museum) and expelled most of its militant unions as Communist-dominated. Many observers trace the disastrous decline of organized labor that continues into the twenty-first century to that decision.

The Left responded to the 1948 Vanport Flood with the Citizens' Disaster Committee D21 that demanded quicker and more generous assistance to flood victims, many of whom were black. Although by that time Portland's leftists were already coming under heavy pressure from the growing McCarthyite movement, they nevertheless continued to lead the local struggle for racial justice through groups like the Oregon Civil Rights Congress. In fact, the Communist Party was the most fully integrated organization in Portland at the time

The low point of the McCarthy Era in Portland came in 1954 with the hearings of the House Un-American Activities Committee (HUAC) D32. A handful of informers named about forty-five Oregonians as Reds—most of whom lost their jobs unless they cooperated with the inquisitors. Four of them, known as the Portland Four D33, were convicted of contempt of court. By the end of the decade, McCarthyism had forced Portland's Old Left into an almost exclusively defensive position when liberal groups joined the McCarthyites by refusing to cooperate with leftists, even when they presumably shared objectives.

With radicals on the defensive, the role of attorneys willing and able to defend them became especially important. In addition to their dean, Irvin Goodman C20, among those who stood up were Reuben Lenske, Nels Peterson, Leo Levenson, Gerald Robinson, and Berkeley Lent.

 Arthur Boose

An old Wobbly, **Arthur Boose**, stood on the corner of **W. Burnside and 3rd Avenue** selling the Industrial Workers of the World (IWW) paper, *The Industrial Worker*, every Saturday for years through the 1940s. He was an energetic landscape painter. In 2004, a posthumous exhibit of newly discovered work was held at Artspace, a Bay City gallery on the Oregon Coast. Prominent Oregon writer Stewart Holbrook attended his funeral.

② Woody Guthrie

At the back of the four-unit house at **6111 SE 92nd Avenue** is the apartment where the iconic folksinger **Woody Guthrie** lived during May and June of 1941. While there, he composed "Roll On Columbia" and twenty-five other songs as an "information consultant" for the Bonneville Power Administration ("Roll On" originally included the politically incorrect line: "We [white settlers] hung every Injun with smoke in his gun"). When Woody left Portland in June,[3] his wife Mary stayed on to party, and it was here that their marriage ended. Woody returned to Portland that September with PETE SEEGER F14, and they sang together at several union halls. In 1947, Michael Loring arranged a concert for Woody at Reed College. His final visit came in 1954 when, ill and destitute, he hitchhiked through town and was jailed as a vagrant that night in Olympia, Washington.

In 1967, while Woody was in a hospital, Interior Secretary Stewart Udall sent him a commendation honoring him for his twenty-eight Columbia River songs and announced that the BONNEVILLE POWER ADMINISTRATION HOOD RIVER SUBSTATION F23 would be named in his honor "in recognition of the fine work you have done to make our people aware of their heritage and the land."

③ *Oshu Nippo* & Oyama Iwao

On December 7, 1941, the FBI raided the offices of the Japanese-language weekly paper **Oshu Nippo** in the Merchant Hotel on **NW Davis between 2nd and 3rd Avenues**. The feds arrested its editor **Oyama Iwao** and confiscated its typesetting equipment. Today, the Oregon Nikkei Legacy Center is located in the building at **117 NW 2nd Avenue**.

④ Minoru Yasui

In March 1942, **Minoru Yasui**, the first Japanese American to graduate from the University of Oregon Law School, was working late in his office in the Foster

Hotel Building at **NW 2nd Avenue and Davis Street**. Determined to challenge a curfew order against persons of Japanese ancestry, he went into the street and demanded that the first police officer he saw arrest him. One officer declined, telling him, "Go home, sonny," but police headquarters finally obliged. He was tried, convicted and sentenced to the Rocky Butte jail. He was later sent to a concentration camp, where Yasui became an FBI informant and supported the persecution of camp inmates who refused to sign loyalty oaths.

 1942 Internment of Japanese Americans

In February 1942, congressional hearings were held at the Federal Court House at **555 SW Yamhill Street** in Portland on the need to deport Japanese American Oregonians to the camps. In contrast to significant opposition at the San Francisco and Seattle hearings, only one isolated voice was raised against the morality of the proposed deportations. It was that of **Azalia Emma Peet** of Gresham, a former Christian missionary in Japan. Peet asked, "What is it that makes it necessary to for them to evacuate? Have they done anything? Is there anything in the history of this area to justify such a fear of them developing overnight?" She went on to challenge the need to deport the "law abiding, upright people of our community." The rest of Portland's religious, liberal, and radical communities were silent. After the deportations, Portland attorney John Kendall managed funds and property for some of the deportees and preserved parts of their properties for their release.

So from May to September of 1942, the animal barns of the **Pacific International Livestock Exposition Building** at **2060 N. Marine Drive** served as a temporary concentration camp for four thousand three hundred Japanese American Oregonians forcibly taken from their homes in Oregon west of Highway 97 and elsewhere in the Northwest. The livestock building occupied the site until the Expo Center replaced it in 1995.

One inmate recalled the horror of "the humiliation and the feeling of being treated like an animal.

You couldn't stand it, the heat and the smell."[4] Another remembered gazing at the bright lights and hearing the noise of the former Jantzen Beach Amusement Park outside the barbed wire. Four inmates died before the rest (including the young Bill Naito) were transported to a permanent camp in Minidoka, Idaho, and elsewhere. In 1946, the first priority of the Oregon Civilian Production Administration was the restoration of the facilities to hold animals again.

 Robert & Carl Deiz

Brothers **Robert (Ruby) and Carl Deiz**, both graduates of Franklin High School, were among the twelve black pilots from Oregon who became "Tuskegee Airmen"—the only black military pilots in World War II. The pilots were named for their training center in Alabama. Robert flew ninety-three missions in the European theater with the segregated 332nd Fighter Group and was the model for a 1943 War Bond poster, one of the few depicting a black person, which was distributed nationwide by the Treasury Department.

Robert and Carl were the sons of William and Elnora Deiz, who lived at **2254 SE 35th Place**. Their father came to Portland in 1914 to work as a waiter at the Portland Hotel and in 1923 became a dining car steward in charge of the Portland to Chicago run. Carl, the younger of the two brothers, married MERCEDES LOPEZ E1 in 1949.

Another Tuskegee airman, Charles Duke, became Portland's first black policeman hired under civil service. A veteran of the 100th Fighter Squadron, Duke lived at **7214 NE 9th Avenue**.

 Sam Markson & the Portland Sign Painters Union

The radical **Sam Markson** came to Portland from New York to work in the shipyards during World War II. After the war, he returned to his earlier trade as a sign painter, lived at **2924 NE 24th Avenue**, and was elected leader of the **Portland Sign Painters Union**. He refused to cooperate with the HUAC D32 witch-hunt in 1954 and was forced out of his union office in retaliation. Markson died in Portland in 1996.

 8 ## The Red Fort & Lieutenant Nicholai Redin

The Red Fort (or "Little Kremlin") was Portland's nickname for the former Wilcox mansion and Rubenstein School of Music at **931 SW King Avenue** in which the Russian Purchasing Agency rented space during World War II. The Soviet Union and the United States were allies against the fascists at the time, and Portland was a major port for shipping supplies to the USSR. Some of the ships built in the Kaiser yards were leased to the Soviets. Originally launched with local names, they were renamed by their new operators. For example, the ship originally named the *Henry L. Corbett* became the Soviet *Alexander Minsky*. Future Senator Richard Neuberger described the scene: "Old–line Portlanders peered in awe from behind their brocaded curtains as the seafaring amazons [Soviet female ship captains] trudged in and out of the brownstone mansion the Soviet purchasing mission had taken over." On other hand, Portlanders more supportive of our wartime ally organized the Russian American Club to entertain Soviet ship crews. After the war, a FBI informer (evidently erroneously) accused future Federal Judge Gus Solomon of belonging to it.[5] In April 1945, a Soviet seaman got drunk while on shore leave in Portland and hanged himself on board his ship, the *Drzuba* (friendship).

After the war, the United States charged one of the Portland purchasing staff, **Soviet Navy Lt. Nicholai Redin**, with espionage. He was acquitted after a trial in which he was defended by IRVIN GOODMAN C20. We know that the FBI kept watch on the Red Fort because, when its reports became public many years later, they noted that then-Portland resident Regina Fischer, the mother of chess champion Bobby Fischer, had applied for a job with the agency and had joined the Communist Party in Portland in 1945. Bobby was two years old at the time.

9 · The Japanese American Cemetery

The Japanese American Cemetery at *NE 50th Avenue and Fremont Street* was the scene of American Legion and police threats against pacifists on August 14, 1943. Portlanders organized by the pacifist Fellowship of Reconciliation planned to clean up the cemetery for observation of the annual *bon matsuri* memorial for the dead by fellowship President Rev. J. W. Reed. Inmates of the concentration camp at Minidoka, Idaho, where most JAPANESE AMERICANS D5 from Portland had been sent, had donated $30 to help pay for supplies needed for the clean-up. But Portland Post No. 1 Commander Joe DeBoest confronted Fred Willits and his cleanup crew at the gate of the cemetery, declared, "The American Legion won't stand for this monkey business," and started pushing Willits away from the gate. He was backed by Portland Police RED SQUAD F26 Captain J. J. Keegan, who yelled, "That's the stand, Commander," and Multnomah County Sheriff Martin Pratt (Pratt had demanded the previous December that all Japanese Americans in Multnomah County pay their property taxes in advance because their property "will have disappeared before the close of another year"). Willits, supported by J. J. Hansaker, countered with, "We're here in a peaceful way and want no trouble for anyone," and said that "99 percent of Fellowship of Reconciliation members are active in Christian churches." Sheriff Pratt finally foiled the would-be clean-up by threatening the religious pacifists with arrest if they tried to enter the cemetery.

 ### 10 · The Negro Shipyard Organization for Victory & the Boilermakers Union 📷

The Negro Shipyard Organization for Victory at the Kaiser shipyards protested their segregation from white members into the local union's auxiliary in 1943. Arnold Beichman, then a reporter for the New York newspaper *PM*, claims that he exposed the Jim Crow practices of the **Boilermakers Union** in 1943 when he interviewed Boilermakers president Tommy Ray. Ray defended his

D: World War II–1960
McCarthyism & Cold War

racist policy by accusing Negro workers of having been used as scabs in a 1919 Portland shipyard strike. U.S. military intelligence considered the Negro Organization to be a "Communist front" and identified its president, Julius Rodriguez, and vice president, Walter Karrington of being "colored members of the Communist Party."[6]

 11 Clara Peoples & Juneteenth 1944

Shipyard worker **Clara Peoples** organized the first **Juneteenth** celebration at the World War II Kaiser shipyards on June 19, 1944. Juneteenth commemorates the day when word of the Emancipation Proclamation reached slaves in Texas, from where Peoples and other shipyard workers had come. After the Vᴀɴᴘᴏʀᴛ Fʟᴏᴏᴅ D21, she and Alene Grice became the first black elevator operators at the Eastern Department store. Peoples lived at *1406 NE Ainsworth Street* and regularly participated in Portland Juneteenth observances.

 12 William H. McClendon

D: World War II–1960
McCarthyism & Cold War

William H. McClendon (1916–1996) lived at *2017 N. Williams Avenue* after he came to Portland from Morehouse College in Atlanta in 1938. In that year he founded one of Portland's most militant black newspapers, *The Portland Observer*, later the *People's Observer*, and finally *The Observer*, which continued until 1950 (a different paper with the same name founded in 1970 still continues publication). McClendon published a letter from "A Few Disgusted Negro Students" from Jefferson High School students in 1944 charging that they were told "NO jitterbugging was allowed" at a school dance but that if they went to "a place designated for [them]…[they] could dance as [they] pleased." McClendon denounced the wartime racist policies of Tommy Ray's Bᴏɪʟᴇʀᴍᴀᴋᴇʀs Uɴɪᴏɴ D10 and supported the Pʀᴏɢʀᴇssɪᴠᴇ Pᴀʀᴛʏ D25 in 1948. He also operated McClendon's Cafe and Jazz Club, directed the Reed College Black Studies Program, and was Portland's National Association for the Advancement of Colored People (NAACP) leader in 1945. In 1943, military intelligence considered Mc-Clendon a "Communist Party organizer." It noted that his *People's Observer* "champions the Negro cause and protests the 'Jim Crow' aspect of Negro union affiliations," and that it was distributed through the Victory Bookstore and other Communist-front establishments.

 13 Gypsy Exodus 1944

When upwards of one hundred **gypsies left Portland** for Texas at the end of 1944, it marked a success for Mayor Earl Riley's campaign of ethnic cleansing. He claimed the gypsies had come to Portland for war work but operated disreputable fortune telling scams in vacant storefronts. Although the police and the Federal Security Agency, which maintained surveillance, reported that "there has never been a case of gypsy women being prostitutes although they may use the ruse to get a victim for fortune telling." Nevertheless, Riley persuaded *The Oregonian* to editorialize "Gypsy, go away" because "A gypsy is always a gypsy, and a gypsy is always a problem."[7] In order to deport his target population out of town, Riley had to procure a special ration of gas from the federal Office of Price Administration sufficient to fuel gypsy trailers all the way to Texas. Before the exodus, the deportees were called to gather at one of their homes at **616 NW 10th Avenue**.

 14 Dr. Ruth Barnett

Naturopathic doctor **Ruth Barnett** (1892–1969) became a leading Portland abortionist when the city was a major center for women's health. She was trained by Dr. Alys Bixby Griff, who lived on the same floor as Barnett and Dʀ. Mᴀʀɪᴇ Eǫᴜɪ B6 in the Oregon Hotel on **SW Broadway and Stark Street**. In 1945, Barnett took over the clinic of Dr. Edgar Stewart, which occupied the entire eleventh floor of *The Oregonian*-owned Broadway Building at **715 SW Morrison Street**. She was arrested and jailed several times in the 1950s but maintained her belief in women's choice throughout her life. Her later offices were in the Jamaica Motel in downtown Portland, on SE McLoughlin Boulevard in Milwaukie, and at her home, which still stands at **2871 SW Champlain Drive**.

 15 Waddles' Restaurant & The Coon Chicken Inn

One of architect Pietro Belluschi's lesser-known buildings in Portland was his 1946 **Waddles' Restaurant** near the Oregon side of the Interstate Bridge. Until its closing in 2004, Waddles' displayed its original slogan, "It's Time to Eat," on its prominent clock. But for blacks it was never time to eat at Waddles' or at many other Portland restaurants and businesses. **The Coon Chicken Inn** at **5474 NE Sandy Boulevard** flaunted its racist façade for several decades until the early 1950s.[8] In 2004, it was bought by Clyde Jenkins who renamed it Clyde's Prime Rib. Jenkins is black and was aware of its history. According to retired Pullman steward Marcus Gordy, until 1938 the bronze drinking fountain at the south end of Union Station also displayed a "Whites Only" sign. In the early 1950s, students from Portland organized a Fair Rose campaign, posting a decal at businesses that pledged not to discriminate.

16 Young Democrats of Multnomah County

In July 1946, the **Young Democrats of Multnomah County** organized a picnic at Blue Lake Park, but park manager Mrs. Paul Keeney barred three of the members because they were black. When the group protested her racist action, Mrs. Keeney charged them with political partisanship and "stirring up racial prejudice." Young Democrat president Hugh Platt replied, "We do not urge the Negro people of Oregon to submit meekly to the established dictates of an intolerant few. We shall fight discrimination wherever we find it. And if that be 'stirring up racial prejudice,' Mrs. Keeney will have to make the most of it." A month later Platt was joined by the county Young Republicans at the Shattuck School to organize a "committee on civic unity" that would identify and act against racial discrimination. They were joined by representatives of the Urban League, NAACP, METHODIST FEDERATION FOR SOCIAL ACTION D37, the Brotherhood of Sleeping Car Porters, the American Veteran's Committee (by BOB CANON D32), the North Chapter of the Inter-Racial Fellowship, the Gona Street Community Club, and even American Legion Post 134 (by Herbert Schwab). They planned to name a citizen of Nisei and one of Chinese ancestry to the board at a later date.

 17 The Portland Roses & Jesse Owens

The famous Olympic champion **Jesse Owens** (1913–1980) owned a black baseball team, the **Portland Roses** (sometimes called the Rosebuds) in 1946 at a time when the AAA Pacific Coast League Portland Beavers would only hire players who could at least "pass for white." The Roses were joined in the West Coast Negro Baseball Association by teams from Seattle, San Francisco, Oakland, Los Angeles, and San Diego. After opening against the Los Angeles White Sox at the Beaver's *NW Vaughn Street* ballpark on June 4, the Roses played only about a dozen games before the new League collapsed at the end of July. On June 23, at the Vaughn Street Park, Owens ran one hundred yards against time, gave a low hurdle exhibition, and raced four team members around the bases.

 18 Brigadier General Evans F. & Peggy Carlson

U.S. Marine Corps Brigadier General Evans F. Carlson (1896–1947) enlisted in the Corps in Portland in 1922 and returned to live in Brightwood, Oregon, after World War II. He died at Legacy Emmanuel Hospital in 1947. He became a national hero for leading his Carlson's Raiders in one of the first assaults on a Japanese-held island in the Pacific early in the war. General Carlson popularized the slogan "Gung Ho" while assigned to China as President Roosevelt's personal correspondent in the 1930s. This slogan, which means "work together," was used by the Chinese People's Liberation Army. Because of his support for the Chinese Revolution and for his membership in the U.S. Committee for a Democratic Far Eastern Policy, he, like Army General "Vinegar Joe" Stillwell, became a victim of McCarthyism.

After his death, his widow, **Peggy Carlson**, who died in 1987, remained in Portland and was the Progressive Party D25 candidate for Congress in 1948. In 1996, the Commandant of the Marine Corps, General C. C. Krulak, sent a glowing testimonial to a celebration of General Carlson's one hundredth birthday held by the Portland chapter of the Evans Carlson Friends of the Peoples Republic of China. Krulak announced that the Marines, after decades of embarrassment, have rehabilitated the "Red General" and have joined China in claiming him as one of their own.

Wardell Henderson

Wardell Henderson, a black war veteran, was executed in 1948 despite broad public protest that his trial was unfair. Accused of killing a white man in Vanport in 1945, Henderson was defended by Irvin Goodman C20, to whom he expressed his thanks and maintained his innocence in his last letter. "The Negro race shall never forget the massive injustice that was done to me," he wrote Goodman. "A lot of people are wondering how I can hold up after such injustice. Well I'll tell you why. It is because I am innocent."[9]

Portland College Student Protests 1948

About two hundred students from five Portland area colleges held a meeting at the Jewish Community Center F19 to protest President Truman's call for a Cold War draft in March 1948. Addressed by famed calligrapher Lloyd Reynolds D32, supported by the local Progressive Citizens of America, and led by Reed student (and future music professor) Bob Crowley, the singing demonstrators marched up Broadway. Vanport, Lewis & Clark, Multnomah College, Reed, the University of Portland, and the Museum Art School were represented.

21 The Citizens' Disaster Committee & the Vanport Flood

The Citizens' Disaster Committee was organized by
Progressive Party D25 supporters—including Nels Peterson,
Vaughn Albertson, Victor Todd, Spencer Gill, Eustus
Curry, and Julia Ruuttila F10—to demand city and state
authorities provide more support to the eighteen thousand people, about one third of whom were black, left
homeless when the Columbia River flood destroyed
the wartime city of **Vanport in 1948**. During the war,
Vanport had been the second largest city in Oregon. The
Committee developed from the Vanport Tenants League
and was supported by, among others, the Oregon Wallace
for President Committee, the Oregon CIO council, and
the Oregon Communist Party. It shared the office of the
American Veterans Committee at **510 SW 2nd Avenue**.
The committee organized a mass meeting at Benson High
School to demand city agencies move faster to provide
unsegregated housing and other services to the flood
refugees. Paul Robeson D40, who had visited Vanport in 1947,
toured the site after the flood and at a Disaster Committee
meeting at the former Holladay School (closed in 1969)
observed "if someone had been more interested in human
life than in profits, this wouldn't have happened." The
Citizens' Committee gave a voice to residents when they
complained to the city council that while business owners
were warned to move their stock, authorities assured
residents that the dikes would hold. Ex-Vanport College
student Bruce Bishop, later editor of the International
Woodworkers of America (IWA) union newspaper, told
the council, "Just give the people of Vanport the chance
to help themselves." A persistent rumor in the black community holds that many more than fifteen people died in
the flood, as was officially reported. The rumors say other
victims were secretly buried in the Terminal Ice and Cold
Storage Company Building at the west end of the Steel
Bridge. As also acknowledged after the 2005 New Orleans
disaster, the Multnomah County Coroner admitted the
possibility that not all bodies had been found. Some, he
said, "may have been carried downriver."

**D: World War II–1960
McCarthyism & Cold War**

The Portland Police RED SQUAD F26, now under the leadership of William "Big Boy" Browne, advised Oregon Governor John Hall to cancel a meeting with the Citizens' Committee because it was a subversive organization. Julia Ruuttila was fired from her job at the Oregon Public Welfare Commission because of her support for the objectives of the Committee and related activities.

 ## 22 The Egyptian Theater

Until recently, the former **Egyptian Theater's** decorative facade remained at *2517 NE MLK Boulevard*. In 1948, black movie patron A. N. Johnson demanded his fifty cents back when theater manager W. Graeper told him blacks were admitted only to the balcony and that he "couldn't buy a seat downstairs." Johnson was among the speakers at a meeting held in the Galilee Baptist Church to plan a campaign to end segregation in Portland theaters and also promote a municipal civil rights ordinance. Other participants included Edwin Berry of the Urban League (who later became its national leader), IRVIN GOODMAN C20, Eustus Curry, who was a PROGRESSIVE PARTY D25 legislative candidate, the NAACP, Oregon Civil Rights Congress, and the Frederick Douglass's club of the Progressive Party. The Hal Spring Club of Oregon's Communist Party (named for a comrade in the LINCOLN BRIGADE C27 who was later killed as a GI in Italy) organized a picket line around the theater, which briefly succeeded in persuading Mr. Graeper to abandon his Jim Crow policy. However, a counter-boycott by white moviegoers caused it to shut down for several weeks.

Goodman's draft of an anti-discrimination ordinance gathered broad support and was passed by the city council in February 1950, when Portland became only the second United States city to outlaw racial discrimination in public accommodations. But, reflecting a dominant racist atmosphere in Portland, voters defeated it in a referendum.

The late Hollywood actor Paul Winfield recalled that he first became aware of racial discrimination in Portland's segregated theaters in the late 1940s.[10]

The First Kaiser Permanente Clinic

The **first Kaiser Permanente clinic** in Portland was established in 1948 at **NE Broadway Street and 26th Avenue**. Part of the postwar Kaiser Permanente was originally founded in Vancouver in 1945. When the wartime Kaiser facilities in the Portland-Vancouver area closed, five former physicians—Charles Grossman, Morris Malbin, Ernest Saward, Wallace Neighbor, and Walter Noehren—decided to try operating the Kaiser hospital and clinic under what was then a controversial pre-paid group practice plan. ABRAHAM LINCOLN BRIGADE C27 veterans Dr. Bernard Malbin and his wife Virginia joined them the following year. By 1950, opposition from the Multnomah County Medical Society to Kaiser Permanente as "socialized medicine" caused many potential members to stay away. But the mass enrollment of one thousand five hundred families from Harry Bridges' INTERNATIONAL LONGSHORE AND WAREHOUSE UNION (ILWU) C9 saved the fledging nonprofit HMO (by 1952, 25 percent of their members were ILWU members). During the McCarthy Era, Kaiser Permanente lost two of its founders, Drs. Grossman and Malbin, when Dr. Saward claimed to rid it of "Marxists and Communists." Now a major health care provider in the Portland area, one of its physicians was elected president of the previously hostile Multnomah County Medical Association in 1996. And Dr. Grossman, one of the few Oregon physicians still in solo private practice, was honored at Grand Rounds at Emmanuel Hospital in 2005.

D: World War II–1960
McCarthyism & Cold War

 ### The Portland School Board & the Left

Portland school buildings were often rented by organizations of the local left, so those seeking to support McCarthyism after World War II by suppressing political assembly pressured the Portland School Board to restrict its use to what it considered politically correct events. The issue came to a head in July 1948, when a member of the board, red baiter and *Oregon Labor Press* editor S. Eugene Allen, moved to bar any organization listed as "subversive" from renting or using any school property. Instead, Allen's colleagues, whom *The Oregonian* reported had just "spent an hour and half listening to members of the audience call each Communists," voted 6–1 to prevent the Oregon Civil Rights Congress from using the Irvington School at **1320 NE Brazee** to hear German Red Gerhard Eisler. But when Allen's proposal came up at next month's meeting the board supported it 4–3 and later even Carey McWilliams was barred.

25 The Progressive Party & Redmen Hall

The Progressive Party, which represented the last major political effort of the U.S. Left in the 1930s, had its 1948 Oregon headquarters in the appropriately named **Redmen Hall**. Its national vice-chair, Paul Robeson D40, attended the organizing convention of the Oregon Progressive Party in 1948, staying at the home of Thomas Moore, the party's secretary, at **5112 SW Maplewood Road**. The convention nominated the national ticket of former Vice President Henry Wallace and Senator Glen Taylor (D-Idaho) to run against the Republicans, Democrats, and Dixiecrats. Several nominees for the Oregon legislature later won Democratic primary elections in Multnomah County. But all were defeated when Wallace-Taylor drew only fifteen thousand votes for President state-wide. Many attribute the failure to attacks in the press charging that the Progressive Party was supported by the Communist Party. When asked about the turnout for one of his campaign stops at the Civic Auditorium in Portland, Wallace said, "Pretty good, considering Portland." His interviewer, a speech-writer friend, claimed his Portland appearance was "organized by a Communist-led union." "Well," Wallace observed, "they get out the crowds."[11] In September, *The Oregonian* made fun of Taylor, a former vaudevillian and still a slick guitar player, by telling readers he "clowned and orated through a two-hour-long speech at a Benson High School" during which he was "showered with flowers from women party followers." Perhaps the paper's editors were responding to Taylor's blaming "scare headlines" for the "current wave of anti-Communist hysteria sweeping the country."

By 1952, only 3,665 Oregonians voted for Vincent Hallinan and Charlotta Bass, the Progressive Party's last national ticket.

 Roy Norene

Between 1949 and 1952, the notorious Portland immigration service officer **Roy Norene**, who had earlier participated with the RED SQUAD F26 in the failed effort to deport ILWU leader Harry Bridges, arrested ten foreign-born Portlanders for belonging to radical groups and recommended their deportation. They included Hamish MacKay, William Mackie, Karolina Halverson, John Stenson, James Yecny (who was arrested at his home at 121 SW 7th Avenue), and Casimiro Absolor. Norene succeeded in deporting MACKAY D42 and MACKIE D43 in 1960 despite the efforts of the OREGON COMMITTEE FOR PROTECTION OF THE FOREIGN BORN D43.

 The Dalles Pineapple Beef 1949

During the ILWU's 1949 Hawaiian strike, in an event known as **"The Dalles Pineapple Beef,"** one ship loaded with pineapples made it to the West Coast but was turned away as "hot cargo" by longshoremen in Seattle and Tacoma. The ship's owners tried to sneak it down the Columbia River in the fog to non-union The Dalles, but the Portland local was alerted and sent hundreds of pickets to prevent unloading. When a strikebreakers' truck almost killed some longshoremen, it was attacked, overturned and its two scabs beaten. One of them was about to be killed when Toby Christenson, a fighter veteran of the 1934 MARITIME STRIKE C9, saved him by knocking his fellow longshoreman out. The longshoremen threw most of the "hot" pineapples in the river and the Hawaiian Pineapple company later won damages from the ILWU. But two scab truckers got their pineapples into Portland and were about to load them into boxcars at the Southern Pacific freight depot at **NW 8th Avenue**

and Hoyt Street when they were caught and set upon
by six ILWU pickets who had eluded police guards. *The
Oregonian* reported that the "fisticuffs climaxed a day of
tension in which heavily armed squads of city police and
state patrolmen sought to protect the two truckers, who
were threatened repeatedly by a group of twenty-five to
forty pickets who followed the trucks in a game of hide
and seek around Portland's west side as they sought a safe
haven to unload."

 28 Allan Hart & The American Civil Liberties Union

Liberal attorney **Allan Hart** (1909–2002), together with
Gus Solomon and others, was one of the authors of a
definitive 1938 expose of the Police RED SQUAD F26, produced by the Oregon chapter of the National Lawyers
Guild. But by 1951, when some Portlanders attempted
to revive a chapter of the **American Civil Liberties
Union (ACLU)** to resist McCarthyism, Hart worked to
prevent it, claiming that some of its proponents, such
as Reuben Lenske and Nels Peterson, wanted it to
become a front for the radical Civil Rights Congress. In
November, Hart reported to the national ACLU office
that thirty people attended a meeting in the Dekum
Building at **519 SW 3rd Avenue** and debated whether
to establish (or revive) a local chapter, and that it was
defeated in a 15–15 tie vote. Ironically, it was the liberal
opposition to its leftist supporters that assured there
would be no ACLU in Portland during the critical
McCarthy Era.

 29 Rose Leopold & the Rosenbergs

Rose Leopold (1918–1995) arrived in Portland in 1951,
a 33-year-old New Yorker who had joined the Communist Party as a college student in the 1930s. She
immediately plunged into local political activism by
organizing a local committee in an effort to save Julius
and Ethel Rosenberg from execution. She recalled that
"the Jewish community was silent all over. They were
scared shitless. Bernie (my husband) and I rented a big

house [**1319 SE 32nd Place**] which became the center for the committee and our events…There was nothing else you could do in those times. The speakers spoke mostly at homes…We all expected the FBI. I knew my phone was tapped…The FBI did come to the door but I said 'I'm not talking to you.'" After the Rosenbergs' execution, Leopold wrote to supporters that the Rosenbergs' "integrity and splendor of purpose inspires the humanist, the progressive, and the radicals of this nation to continue the fight to clear their good name. We on this Committee to Secure Justice in the Rosenberg Case will do that and more." She continued to host leftist speakers and write protest letters against McCarthyism to the Portland papers. When HUAC D32 came to town in 1954 she observed with sorrow that "there was such a terrible, dead silence…One weekend every progressive I knew went to the beach. They thought they might be called." Later, Leopold was active in the WOMEN'S INTERNATIONAL LEAGUE FOR PEACE AND FREEDOM (WILPF) B18, the DoJump Theater, Red Rose School, and *The Portland Alliance*.[12]

 30 Guild Theater & Censorship

For many years the **Board of Motion Picture and Entertainment Review** tried to keep Portlanders away from radical films. In 1940, for example, they banned the Soviet movie, *Doctor Malmock*, which told the story of a Jewish doctor in Nazi Germany who fled to the Soviet Union. It was banned because the Board found it "offensive to a friendly power,"—Nazi Germany! One Reed student, Jerome Radding, signed a petition protesting the ban and fifteen years later, as a doctor in a veteran's hospital, he was branded a security risk for his protest.[13] The censor board finally overstepped its bounds in 1953, after its effort to ban DeSica's classic, *The Bicycle Thief*, from showing at the **Guild Theater** at **1219 SW Park Avenue** was overturned by the courts. In the 1930s, the Guild's predecessor, the Studio Theater, was prevented by the censors from showing newsreels—previously not subject to review. Noting that the board members had found twenty-four objectionable scenes in the 1,853 films they had watched in the past two years, the board told the city council that "The cost in time and money [$5,000 annually] is too great for the results obtained." However in 1960, a state obscenity law allowed Mayor Terry Shrunk to demand that the Guild Theater cut two scenes from Louis Malle's film *The Lovers*. Theater manager Nancy Welch was arrested when she refused and leading Portland cultural figures, including PSU film professor Andries Deinum, protested the censorship.

 31 Dr. George Ebey

Former Portland public school leader **Dr. George Ebey** was hired away to be deputy school superintendent in Houston in 1952, but fired a year later after a Portlander, Virgil Holland, attacked Ebey as "soft on Communism." The Houston school board fired Ebey by a 4–3 vote not for any problems with his performance but because he did not provide enough evidence that he "actively fought" Communism in the American Veterans Committee in California in 1946. Portlanders interviewed by the investigator for the Houston board expressed "indignation and amazement" at "having words put in our mouths" after assuring him that Dr. Ebey did not exhibit any "disloyal" behavior in Portland.

 32 The House Un-American Activities Committee & Lloyd Reynolds 📷

The June 1954 hearings of the **HUAC** were held in what is now known as the Gus Solomon United States Courthouse between *SW 6th Avenue and Broadway*. HUAC's intent, as elsewhere during the McCarthy Era, was to expose and isolate dissident Oregonians. Its main informers were a former Reed College student, Homer Owen, and former Reed Dean of Students, Bob Canon, who together named about forty-five victims—many connected to Reed—as having been members of the Communist Party years before.[14] All of the suspects relied on the constitutional grounds for refusing to respond to interrogation about their political affiliations, and four of them, known as the PORTLAND FOUR D33, were later convicted of contempt of Congress for their defiance. Most of those who refused to cooperate with HUAC were fired from their jobs, including William Lewis at Mitchell Brothers Truck Line and Professor Stanley Moore at Reed College, which also suspended world-renowned calligrapher **Lloyd Reynolds** from teaching his summer art history class. Reynolds refused to answer their political questions, including whether he had "ever made posters, graphic art things, and exhibits of that nature for the Communist Party while at Reed College." The college resisted efforts to reverse its decision to fire Moore for more than thirty years, and it was not until 1997, when Moore could not attend for health reasons, that he was finally invited back to campus. The fear that dominated the McCarthy Era assured there would be little protest in Portland (with the exception of the academic components of Reed College) against HUAC. There was NO ACLU CHAPTER D28, but ironically, seventy members of the Multnomah County Young Republican Club, meeting in March at the Chamber of Commerce offices, voted unanimously to condemn "the investigation methods" of Senator McCarthy.

 The Portland Four

The Portland Four, who lost their jobs, were arrested, and convicted of contempt of Congress after refusing to cooperate with HUAC D32, were Herbert Simpson, a clerk at Inland Motor Freight; Donald Wollam, a part-time longshoreman; Tom Moore, a farm-supply businessman; and John MacKenzie, an assistant produce manager at Fred Meyer. In trials at today's Gus Solomon building, they were convicted because the politically biased Judge George Boldt basically directed the jury to deliver a guilty verdict. They were all fired or lost their businesses, and their families endured years of harassment and unemployment, even though the charges were dropped in 1957 after three of them appealed to the U.S. Supreme Court, where the Justice Department admitted it made a mistake in prosecuting them. The Portland Four are all deceased, but each has some family members living in Portland.[15]

 The Families of the Portland Four

The families of the PORTLAND FOUR D33 were also victims of the McCarthy Era. The widow of John MacKenzie described the "crisis atmosphere" that permeated their "fortress home" at **6125 SE 86th Avenue**. Mary Mackenzie said they and their children withdrew from all political and most social activity because they feared the FBI and informers like John's fellow Reedie Homer Owen—the source of their troubles when he named John as a Communist before **HUAC** D32.[16] Looking back in 1998, Betty Wollam, widow of Don Wollam, recalled the atmosphere in Portland during the McCarthy Era. As a Communist active in leftist unions, especially the Marine Cooks and Stewards branch at **127 W. Burnside Street,** she noticed that soon after the end of World War II, the local radio and press began giving "virulent anti-Communist sentiments" generous attention. The personal consequence was that "friends who had never said anything to you about your politics began to be a little sharp. Gradually old friends drifted away under pressure. By 1950, I don't believe I had a single friend left."[17] Their daughter, Cate Wollam, remembers that after her father vigorously challenged HUAC in 1954, chalk curses were written in front of their home at **3154 SE Salmon Street** and she couldn't go and play until her parents had "washed the nasty words off the sidewalk." When Tom Moore lost his farm supply business for failing to cooperate with HUAC, his son, Barron Moore, was sent to live on a farm and the family was forced to leave Portland and move to California.[18]

 Michele Russo & William Givler

Portland's most celebrated artist, the late **Michele Russo**, whose studio was at **314 SW 9th Avenue**, was conveniently out of town and thus unable to be subpoenaed to appear before HUAC D32 in 1954, even though he was named as a Red by informer Robert Canon. Russo and his wife, Sally Healy, came to Portland during World War II and lived in Vanport, where he registered as a member of the PROGRESSIVE PARTY D25, until the FLOOD OF 1948 D21. A courageous exception to the behavior of other Portland educational institutions such as Reed College was the Portland Museum Art School (now Northwest College of Art). Its Dean, **William Givler**, himself a prominent artist, defied FBI agents who came to warn him about his instructor's politics and defended Russo's right to continue teaching there.

 ### The Hunters & the Portland Realty Board

Despite having $2,000 for a down payment, when Navy petty officer **George Hunter** and his wife **Frances** tried to buy a home in the northeastern suburbs of Portland in 1955, their offers were all refused. Finally, the president of the **Portland Realty Board**, Charles Paine, cleared up the issue. The Hunters were black and the three hundred and sixty realtors in Portland had a "code of ethics which prohibits them from selling houses in white districts," he admitted, "without the consent of the neighbors."

 ### The Methodist Federation for Social Action & Reverend Mark Chamberlain

The Methodist Federation for Social Action (MFSA) in Gresham was led by the **Reverend Mark Chamberlain**, who was also a leader in the OREGON COMMITTEE FOR THE DEFENSE OF THE FOREIGN BORN D43 and participated in the ILWU'S BLOODY THURSDAY C9 commemorations. The MFSA was one of the few centers of resistance during the bleak McCarthy years of the 1950s. Through meetings, pamphlets, and preaching, Reverend Chamberlain, his wife, and a small group of committed Methodists and others provided a venue for dissenters and their causes. The federation's Sunday evening worship services and lecture programs were held at its meeting hall, *1910 NE Davis*

Street, and occasionally would use the larger venue of the CENTENARY WILBUR METHODIST CHURCH F2.

 The Friendly Forum

The Friendly Forum, which met in the cafeteria of the old YMCA building downtown, also provided an opportunity to hear dissenters during the McCarthy Era by holding regular lunches to hear mostly leftist speakers. They included visitors to the city such as artist Rockwell Kent, literary critic Annette Rubenstein, Mrs. Morton Sobell, Julian Schuman, and Ammon Hennacy, but also Portlanders such as attorney Reuben Lenske and peace activist FERN GAGE F20.

 The Oregon Committee to Halt Nuclear Testing

In 1957, **The Oregon Committee to Halt Nuclear Testing** began by distributing pamphlets of Albert Schweitzer's plea against nuclear war to patrons of the GUILD THEATER D30 at 1219 SW Park Avenue, which was then showing a film about Schweitzer, the widely respected missionary and scientist. The committee was one of the first local peace organizations established during the Cold War by E. Wilton Hartzler of the American Friends Service Committee, Phyllis Johansen, wife of painter George Johansen, Helen Gordon of the JEWISH COMMUNITY CENTER F19, and myself, Michael Munk. The group raised funds for a full-page ad in a local newspaper and carried out a downtown petition drive against nuclear bomb testing. The Oregon Committee later joined with the national Committee for a Sane Nuclear Policy (SANE). Among its supporters were Rep. Edith Green, Maureen Neuberger, chemistry professor Arthur Livermore of Reed College, and representatives of the Unitarian, Methodist, and Christian churches.

 Paul Robeson & Senator Mark Hatfield

The last of **Paul Robeson's** many visits to Portland came in 1958 for one of his first public concerts after being blacklisted for his political views. It was sponsored by a leftist student group at Reed College and tickets were sold by The House of Sound, a record store in the heart of the city's black community at **2343 N. Williams Avenue**. Indeed, black Portlanders made up more than one third of the overflow audience of over one thousand, with most of them making their first visit to the college by trolley bus. The enthusiastic support for Robeson from the black community was in sharp contrast to the fear shown by Portland's music establishment (downtown music ticket outlets J. K. Gill and Sherman Clay refused to even display posters of Robeson, who had filled the Civic [now Keller] Auditorium many times before he was blacklisted). On Williams Avenue, the black community's business district, almost every store, bar, and beauty parlor proudly displayed it.

At least one of Robeson's visits to Oregon stirred up racism. Former **Senator Mark Hatfield** recalls that after a Robeson concert at Willamette University in 1942, Robeson and fellow artist Marian Anderson, who died in Portland in 1993 at the home of her nephew, Portland Symphony conductor James DePreist, were barred from staying overnight in any Salem hotels. Hatfield, then a Willamette student, drove Robeson to a Portland hotel—probably the Benson—where Anderson had previously been allowed to stay. Hatfield recalled that a photo of Robeson as a guest of Hatfield's fraternity before the 1942 concert was used by his opponents to red-bait him in the 1950 campaign, his first for the state legislature.

In a 2001 *Oregonian* article, Oregon State University star tailback Ken Simonton picked out Robeson (a star scholar and athlete at Rutgers University) as a "football scholar-baller who endured the nonsense long enough to open doors for a brother like myself...far beyond the playing field."

 Linus Pauling

The only Nobel Laureate awarded two prizes that were not shared with another recipient (Chemistry and Peace), **Linus Pauling** (1900–1994) lived in his mother's boarding house at **3945 SE Hawthorne Boulevard** from 1910 until he went to Oregon State Agricultural College (now Oregon State University) in Corvallis. He performed his first chemistry experiments in its basement while attending Washington High School. At his death, *The Oregonian* anointed Pauling "Oregon's Biggest Brain," but in 1954, during the McCarthy Era it joined much of the media by accusing him of "fuzzy thinking" for defending fellow scientist Robert Oppenheimer against accusations of disloyalty. The Institute for Science, Engineering, and Public Policy hoped to convert the property into a museum devoted to the chemist and peace activist's life and work.

42 Hamish Scott MacKay

At Portland International Airport on the evening of November 18, 1960, **Hamish Scott MacKay** was torn from the arms of his young sons by government agents, put on a plane, and deported to his native Canada. MacKay worked temporary jobs in the Portland area during the Depression, working on farms, in the woods, and in hop and wheat fields. Those experiences gradually radicalized him and he joined the OREGON WORKERS ALLIANCE (OWA) C24. With the OWA, he picketed fascist ships on the Portland docks, joined the protests against the execution of TED JORDAN C5, and read Communist publications.

The long saga of MacKay's deportation began in 1936 when, while working on the Works Progress Administration (WPA) stream protection project on Johnson Creek, ROY NORENE D26, head of the Portland office of the U.S. Immigration Service, came to MacKay's home at **5425 SE Henderson Street**, demanding to know whether he was a Communist.[19] However, Norene did not succeed in deporting MacKay until the McCarthy Era provided a more supportive environment.

Later, with the support of Oregon senators Morse and Hatfield, MacKay was free to return to Portland, but preferred to live in Vancouver, B.C., while making frequent visits to family and friends in Portland. Before his death in 1984, he asked to be buried at Skyline Memorial Gardens, **4101 SW Skyline Boulevard**. A hundred people, many of whom had helped him fight his deportation, attended his funeral. One of his honorary pallbearers was fellow political deportee WILLIAM MACKIE D43.

 ### William Mackie & The Oregon Committee for the Defense of the Foreign Born 📷

The Oregon Committee for Defense of the Foreign Born (sometimes called The Oregon Committee For Protection of the Foreign Born), working from **4616 SW Corbett Street**, was the main support of MACKAY D42 and other deportation targets of the local office of the U.S. Immigration Service. Continuing its role of suppressing dissent from the foreign born in previous Red Scares, the notorious ROY NORENE D26 ordered the arrests of ten Oregonians in 1949 for having belonged to radical groups. In addition to MacKay, the police also arrested another former OWA C24 member, housepainter **William Mackie**, then living at **4326 N. Montana Avenue**, who came to Portland from Finland as a child, and Filipino Casimiro Absolor, an officer of the Cannery Workers Union. Both JULIA RUUTTILA F10 and MARTINA GANGLE CURL F13 were active in the committee.

Mackie and MacKay were the only two among the ten who were eventually deported. Federal Judge Gus Solomon ruled that informers Robert Wilmot, former Portland newspaperman, and retired railroad worker Lee Knipe of Hillsboro, had provided "ample proof Mackie had been a Red," although he acknowledged that the Walter-McCarran Internal Security Act under which he would be deported was a "terrible law." With the help of Oregon senators Wayne Morse and Mark Hatfield, Mackie was allowed to return to Portland in 1976 after promising not to join leftist groups.

D: World War II–1960 McCarthyism & Cold War

World War II–1960 Notes

1. *Daily Peoples' World*, May 4, 1947.

2. Counter Intelligence Branch, G-2, Western Defense Command, Presidio of San Francisco, *Summary of Subversive Situation*. August 1, 1943. (Confidential).

3. When Woody left to hitchhike back East, his first ride along the Columbia River was from attorney and later federal judge Gus Solomon.

4. Interview with Tom Fujita, 2001.

5. Counter Intelligence Branch, G-2, Western Defense Command, Presidio of San Francisco, *Summary of Subversive Situation*. August 1, 1943. (Confidential).

6. Harry H. Stein, Gus J. Solomon, *Liberal Politics, Jews, and the Federal Courts* (Portland, OR: Oregon Historical Society Press, 2007) 74.

7. *The Oregonian*, December 28, 1944. Also see "How Portland Deported its Gypsies During World War II," *The Portland Alliance*, July 2001.

8. This was a chain founded in Salt Lake City in 1925, according to Psyche A. Williams-Forson's *Building Houses Out of Chicken Legs: Black Women, Food, and Power* (Chapel Hill, NC: The University of North Carolina Press, 2006). The book includes accounts of the chain's racist practices by Roy Hawkins, a former waiter.

9. From his letter published in *The Oregonian*, January 25, 1948.

10. *The Oregonian*, March 10, 2004.

11. Michael Straight, *After Long Silence* (New York: W. W. Norton & Co. Inc., 1983).

12. Interview by Sandy Polishuk, *The Portland Alliance*, February 1996.

13. Letter, *Reed Magazine*, November 1997.

14. Michael Munk, "Oregon Tests Academic Freedom in (Cold) Wartime: The Reed College Trustees versus Stanley Moore," *Oregon Historical Quarterly*, Fall 1996.

15. Also see Michael Munk, "McCarthyism Revisited," *Reed Magazine*, May 2006.

16. Mary MacKenzie, "Surviving the McCarthy Era: A Family Perspective," unpublished manuscript, 2006.

17. Interview by Janet Dietz, *The Portland Alliance*, June 1998.

18. See Mary MacKenzie, "Surviving…" for more on the Wollam and Moore families.

19. See excerpts from his diaries, edited by Michael Munk, in Craig Wollner and Tracy Dillon's *A Richer Harvest: The Literature of Work in the Pacific Northwest* (Corvallis, OR: Oregon State University Press, 1999.)

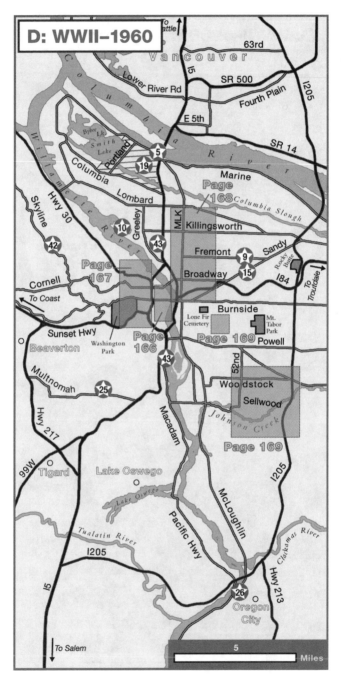

D: WWII–1960

To Seattle

63rd

Vancouver

Lower River Rd

I5

SR 500

Fourth Plain

I205

E 5th

SR 14

Columbia River

Bybee Lk

Smith Lake

Portland

5

19

Marine

Page 168

Columbia Slough

Columbia

Lombard

Willamette River

Hwy 30

Skyline

Greeley

MLK

Killingsworth

42

10

43

Fremont

Sandy

9

15

Rocky Butte

Broadway

I84

To Troutdale

Cornell

Page 167

To Coast

Burnside

Lone Fir Cemetery

Mt. Tabor Park

Sunset Hwy

Washington Park

Page 166

43

Page 169

Powell

Beaverton

Multnomah

25

52nd

Woodstock

Sellwood

Macadam

Johnson Creek

Page 169

Hwy 217

99W

Tigard

Lake Oswego

Lake Oswego

I205

Pacific Hwy

McLoughlin

Tualatin River

I205

I5

Clackamas River

Hwy 213

26

Oregon City

To Salem

5

Miles

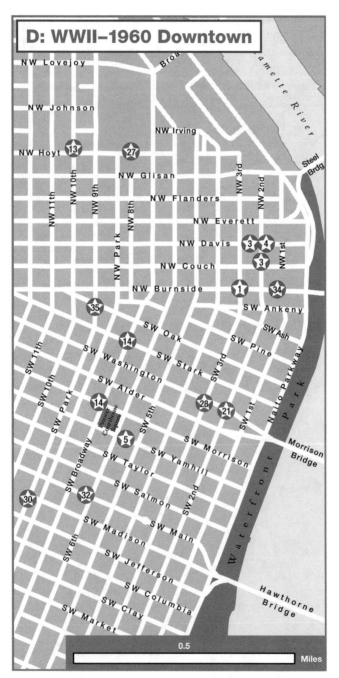

D: WWII–1960 Downtown

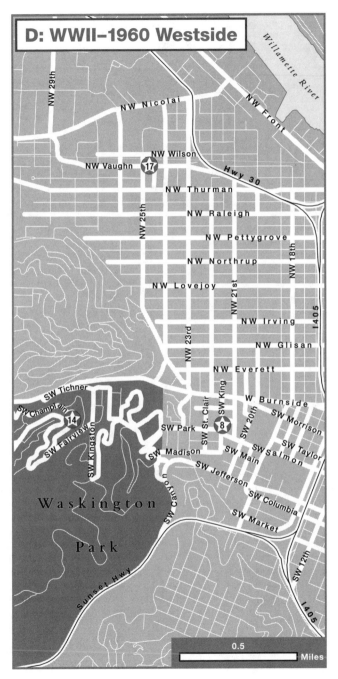

D: WWII–1960 Westside

Willamette River

NW 29th

NW Nicolai

NW Front

NW Wilson

NW Vaughn 17

Hwy 30

NW Thurman

NW 25th

NW Raleigh

NW Pettygrove

NW 18th

NW Northrup

NW Lovejoy

NW 21st

NW Irving

I 405

NW 23rd

NW Glisan

NW Everett

SW Tichner

W. Burnside

SW Champlain

SW St. Clair

SW King

14

SW 20th

SW Morrison

SW Fairview

SW Park

8

SW Taylor

SW Kingston

SW Madison

SW Main

SW Salmon

SW Canyon

SW Jefferson

SW Columbia

Waskington

SW Market

Park

SW 12th

Sunset Hwy

I 405

0.5

Miles

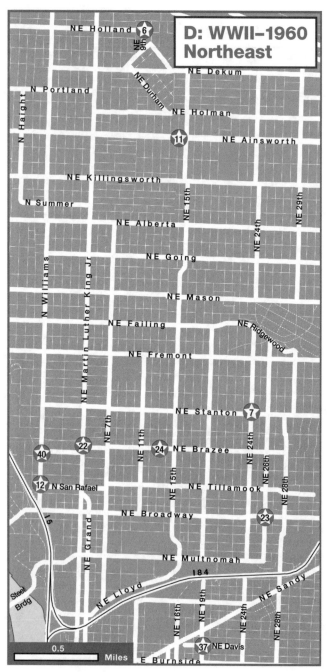

D: WWII–1960
Northeast

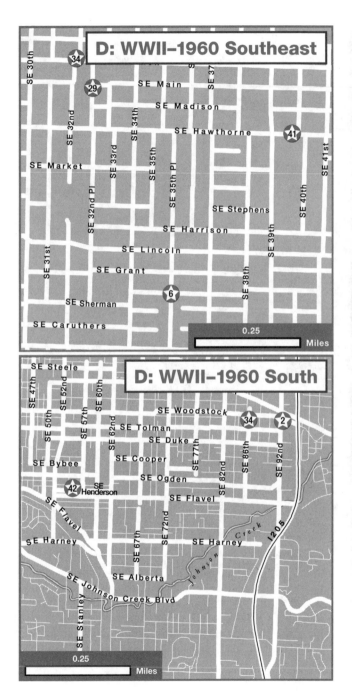

D: WWII–1960 Southeast

SE 30th
34
29
SE Main
SE 37
SE Madison
SE 34th
SE Hawthorne
41
SE 33rd
SE 35th
SE 35th Pl
SE 41st
SE Market
SE 32nd Pl
SE 35th Pl
SE 40th
SE Stephens
SE Harrison
SE 39th
SE 31st
SE Lincoln
SE Grant
SE 38th
6
SE Sherman
SE Caruthers

0.25
Miles

D: WWII–1960 South

SE Steele
SE 47th
SE 52nd
SE 60th
SE Woodstock
34
2
SE 50th
SE 57th
SE 62nd
SE Tolman
SE Duke
SE 77th
SE 86th
SE 92nd
SE Bybee
SE Cooper
SE Ogden
SE 82nd
42 SE Henderson
SE Flavel
SE Flavel
SE 67th
SE 72nd
Johnson Creek
I 205
SE Harney
SE Harney
SE Alberta
SE Johnson Creek Blvd
SE Stanley

0.25
Miles

 Wobbly Arthur Boose sold *The Industrial Worker,* the IWW
newspaper, on the corner of W. Burnside Street and 3rd Avenue
through the 1940s. *Oregon Historical Society, OrHi10695.*

 Woody Guthrie F23 lived at 6111 SE 92nd Avenue while writing his Columbia River songs. The sticker on his guitar reads "This Machine Kills Fascists." *NYWT&S Photograph Collection, Library of Congress, LC-USZ62-130859.*

 Portland's Red Fort, also known as the former Wilcox mansion and Rubenstein School of Music, stands at 931 SW King Avenue. Both the Red Squad F26 and the FBI watched the house for Communist activity after World War II. *Colin Smith.*

Portland's Japanese Americans were interned for the hot summer of 1942 at the animal barns of the Pacific International Livestock Exposition Building on N. Marine Drive. Four inmates died before the others, including a young Bill Naito, were transported to a permanent camp in Idaho. *Oregon Historical Society, OrHi28157.*

Fair Employment
Practice Committee

REQUEST NAMES OF ALL NEGROES DISCHARGED
BY THE KAISER CO., INC.

JULIUS RODRIQUEZ

President of the Shipyard Negro Organization for Victory, recently returned from a Conference in Washington, D. C. Giving a Report at a Meeting

Monday, August 16, 1943

—AT—

HUDSON HOUSE DORMITORY

N. E. LOUNGE A T 7:30 P. M.

If you have been discharged for non-payment of dues, or for refusal to join the Boilermaker's Auxiliary, or if you have been re-employed in the yards, or secured other employment, it makes no difference . . .

PLEASE BE PRESENT

THIS IS A REQUEST OF THE F. E. P. C.

The Negro Shipyard Organization for Victory protested being segregated from the all-white Boilermakers Union. This flier advertised a meeting in August 1943 where President Julius Rodriquez reported on a Washington, D. C., conference he had attended. *City of Portland Archives, A2001-074.*

 Waddles' Restaurant operated from 1946 to 2004 in its prominent location next to the Interstate Bridge. Into the 1950s, a sign on the building read "White Trade Only—Please." *Oregon Historical Society, OrHi29161.*

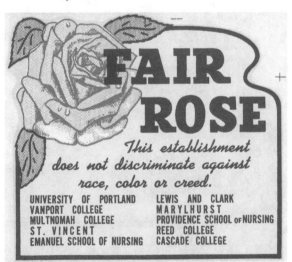

FAIR ROSE

This establishment does not discriminate against race, color or creed.

UNIVERSITY OF PORTLAND	LEWIS AND CLARK
VANPORT COLLEGE	MARYLHURST
MULTNOMAH COLLEGE	PROVIDENCE SCHOOL of NURSING
ST. VINCENT	REED COLLEGE
EMANUEL SCHOOL OF NURSING	CASCADE COLLEGE

 The Fair Rose campaign was started by students in the 1950s. Decals like this one denoted establishments that pledged not to discriminate. *Michael Munk.*

Dr. Ruth Barnett lived in this home at 2871 SW Champlain Drive in the West Hills. *Colin Smith.*

Peggy Carlson ran for Congress in 1948 on the Progressive Party D25 ticket. Her photo was listed along with the rest of the Party's slate of candidates in this flier. *Michael Munk.*

The Vanport Flood of 1948 displaced more than eighteen thousand people, nearly one third of them black, when the Columbia River destroyed the wartime city of Vanport. This photo shows two men, one carrying a small child away from the destruction. *City of Portland Archives, A2001-025.1208.*

The Vanport Flood caused the Progressive Party D25 to organize the Citizens' Disaster Committee to demand more support from city and state officials for those who lost their homes. The Committee was supported by the Oregon CIO and the Communist Party, among others. *City of Portland Archives, A2001-078.*

A Program for Oregon...

- Public Housing Program
- Development of Public Power
- Price Support for Farm Products
- State FEPC Bill
- Repeal of Anti-Labor Laws
- Expanded Educational Opportunities
- Protection of State Timber Lands
- Liberalized unemployment benefits and workman's compensation

PROGRESSIVE
PARTY OF
OREGON

HENRY A. WALLACE
PROGRESSIVE CANDIDATE FOR
PRESIDENT
OF THE UNITED STATES

The Future
Belongs to **YOU**
VOTE PROGRESSIVE IN '48

**PROGRESSIVE
PARTY OF
OREGON**

PEACE-FREEDOM-ABUNDANCE

The Progressive Party represented the last major political effort of the U.S. Left in the 1930s. This pamphlet, from the 1948 presidential season, states the party platform. The presidential ticket of Henry Wallace and Glen Taylor only drew fifteen thousand votes statewide, which some attributed to negative press coverage and attacks claiming a link between progressives and the Communist Party. *Michael Munk*.

 22 The former Egyptian Theater still stands at 2517 NE MLK Boulevard. In 1948, black patron A. N. Johnson demanded his fifty cents back when he was told he could only sit in the balcony. It was many years before Johnson was allowed on the floor. *Colin Smith*.

 29 Rose Leopold was an active Portland radical for nearly fifty years. She organized a committee to save Julius and Ethel Rosenberg and was active in WILPF. Jon Kimball was also identified by the Red Squad F26 in this photo which was taken at a peace rally in February of 1966. *City of Portland Archives, A2004-005*.

 The Guild Theater, at 1219 SW Park Avenue, was the center of a storm over the 1953 censorship of the classic film, *The Bicycle Thief*. It was also the site of radical events from the 1930s to the 1960s. *Colin Smith*.

 Andries Deinum, a film professor at Portland State University, protested censorship of Louis Malle's film, *The Lovers*, in 1960. He came to PSU after being fired by the University of Southern California for being called before HUAC. *Portland State University*.

37 The Reverend Mark Chamberlain led the Methodist Federation for Social Action which became a haven for dissenters and their views. He's shown here at a February 6, 1966, peace rally. *City of Portland Archives, A2004-005.*

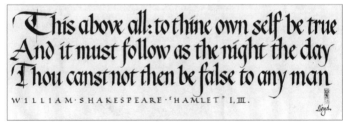

This above all: to thine own self be true
And it must follow as the night the day
Thou canst not then be false to any man
WILLIAM·SHAKESPEARE·'HAMLET'·I,III.

32 Lloyd Reynolds was one of many who refused to answer questions about his political affiliation when called before HUAC D32. This example of his calligraphy, a Shakespeare quotation, was given as a gift to Ruth Freeman Stovall for her $35 donation to *People's World*, the Communist newspaper, in the early 1950s. *Dennis Stovall.*

 Paul Robeson was a favorite of Portland's radical community. This snapshot, taken in March 1958, shows Robeson at his last local concert visit, talking to Dr. Charles Grossman D23, one of the last Portland physicians who still makes house calls. *Charles Grossman.*

 Linus Pauling, the only Nobel Laureate awarded two prizes that were not shared by another recipient, lived in his mother's boarding house at 3945 SE Hawthorne Boulevard. He was called "soft on Communism" by *The Oregonian*. *Library of Congress, LC-USZ62-76925.*

THE EXILE OF
HAMISH MacKAY and
WILLIAM MACKIE

" . . . now he is here, a man without papers or chattels, a
penniless refugee in a borrowed coat . . . "

From Helsinki *Paivan Sanomat*, November 21, 1960

 Hamish Scott MacKay was deported to Canada in 1960 for his
involvement with "radical" organizations in Portland like the OWA
C24. This flier protested his persecution by the Portland red baiters.
Michael Munk.

WILLIAM MACKIE

AN URGENT APPEAL
TO OUR FELLOW AMERICANS

**Help Us to Prevent a World War
Veteran from Being Exiled**

 43

William Mackie was deported due
to the efforts of Roy Norene D26 and
others. He was eventually allowed
to return to Portland with the help
of Senators Morse and Hatfield D40.
This flier tells his story. *Michael
Munk.*

On July 5, 1966, the American Friends Service Committee walked through the streets of Portland with symbolic caskets. They were protesting U.S. involvement in Vietnam, or as they say on the sign, "World War III." Ace Hayes F21 is the pallbearer looking at the camera. *City of Portland Archives, A2004-005.*

E: 1961–1973
Peaceniks & Civil Rights

Portlanders participated vigorously in the two great social and political movements of the decade: the largely non-violent struggle for civil rights against the often violent institutions of racial segregation and discrimination and the frequently angry opposition to the massive U.S. intervention in the Vietnamese Civil War.

One of the few Communists still standing, Susan Wheeler (1942–2006), helped to organize the city's largest civil rights march—eight thousand strong—to protest the 1965 police attacks on Martin Luther King's early march for civil rights in Selma, Alabama. Three years later, Portland's black community expressed its outrage at King's assassination in spontaneous street protests in which Portland police were accused of gratuitous VIOLENCE AGAINST BLACK DEMONSTRATORS E9. The Portland chapter of the militant BLACK PANTHER PARTY (BPP) E10 organized free breakfast, health, and dental programs, but its members were frequently harassed and arrested.

The transformation of earlier efforts for racial justice to the mass movement of the 1960s owed a debt to the Old Left's original efforts, as racists who tried to defeat the struggle acknowledged when they called civil rights leaders Communists. Wheeler and many of her comrades supported the mass movement that they had prepared the ground for their work.

President Lyndon Johnson's administration's full-scale intervention in the Vietnam War in 1964 was endorsed by Congress when it passed the Gulf of Tonkin Resolution on the basis of false information from the Johnson administration. Oregon Senator Wayne Morse was joined only by Alaska's Ernest Gruening in courageously exposing the fraudulent claims and voting against the resolution. Morse was eventually vindicated when the United

States finally "cut and ran" from Vietnam in 1975 bearing responsibility for millions of deaths. Later, Republican SENATOR MARK HATFIELD D40 also opposed the war, as did Oregon Representative Charles O. Porter. Opposition to the Vietnam War in Portland gathered steam through the 1960s but reached a climax in 1970 when students were killed by the National Guard in Mississippi and Ohio, leading to a STUDENT STRIKE AT PORTLAND STATE UNIVERSITY E15 that was also attacked by Portland police. EXPLOSIONS INTENDED TO PROTEST THE WAR E18 occurred in city hall and military recruiting stations in Portland's east side.

If the remnants of the Old Left contributed to the civil rights movements and generally opposed the Vietnam War, leadership of the ultimately successful antiwar movement came primarily from a New Left—composed largely of youth and student groups such as the STUDENTS FOR A DEMOCRATIC SOCIETY (SDS) E5 who had not previously engaged in political activity. Although the SDS had its roots in the old Socialist Party, its revival in the 1960s was distinguished by their refusal to adopt the anti-Communist ethos of their McCarthy Era elders and by their preference for organizing anti-hierarchical community structures rather than electing candidates of a national political party.

Reflecting its distrust of anyone "over 30," the New Left showed little interest in the recommendations of the Old Left but struggled to define a radical ideology of its own. "We need to name that system" that causes wars, racism, and poverty, SDS leader Paul Potter famously declared to its first mass demonstration in 1965. But as an organization it never did, and instead gradually fragmented into feuding groups including some that urged violent confrontation with "The Establishment." Indeed, the roots of many later "identity" movements grew from objections to the straight white males of the New Left's original leadership. On the other hand, the demographics of that leadership reflected accurately the opposition to draft by the war's domestic constituency.

Other new political groups organized in Portland during this period were the Society for New Action Politics (SNAP) and two groups that adopted the

Panther symbol (originally used by an Alabama voting rights effort): the White Panthers (whose house at 3436 SW 1st Avenue was raided in 1970 by police and the FBI) and the older Grey Panthers who continue to be active in Portland.

In February 1970, the SDS-led (and the Student Mobilization Committee-supported) anti-military re-cruiting demonstrations at PSU culminated when about twenty students surrounded two U.S. Navy recruiters in the Smith Memorial Student Union. Four of them, Maureen Gray, Ileana Fenyo (wife of PSU Professor Mario Fenyo), Lynn Meyer, and Dan Wolf made sure the recruiters left the building. For their direct action protest against the Vietnam War, the "PSU Four" were expelled from the University despite efforts of their lawyer DON CHAMBERS F11.

Naturally, the revival of activism in the 1960s caused an expansion of the RED SQUAD F26, whose files were quickly filled with informer reports and photo surveillance of Portlanders exercising their political rights. They kept almost full-time watches at what they called "known militant communes" at SE 47th Avenue and Bybee Boulevard and at SE 22nd Avenue and Ivon Street.

> While the races may stand side by side, whites stand on history's mountain and blacks stand on history's hollow. We must overcome unequal history before we can overcome unequal opportunity.
> —President Lyndon Baines Johnson (shortly before his death in 1973)

 **1** Mercedes Deiz

Before moving to Portland in 1948 and becoming the Northwest's first black judge, **Mercedes Deiz** (1917–2005) was active in the militant American Labor Party in New York as Mercedes Lopez Owens, daughter of a black Cuban father and a white Czech mother. She dated the prominent writer Ralph Ellison during "their salad days" in the late 1930s. "I remember sitting around with wonderful writers like Ellison and [Richard]

E: 1960–1973
Peaceniks & Civil Rights

Wright, listening and learning," she told a Portland interviewer in 1999. "I was so lucky to have that exposure to the great minds of the Harlem Renaissance."[1] She graduated from the Northwest College of Law (now Lewis & Clark Law School), managed Ben Anderson's law office, and in 1960 became the first black woman to be admitted to the Oregon State Bar.

But when she was appointed the same year to the Portland Youth Commission, the RED SQUAD F26 reported that "leading Negro citizens are very displeased with the appointment and a representative of their groups is going to contact the Mayor regarding same." The Red Squad report went on to cite "rumors that she is still secretly in the movement" and that when Deiz was living in New York, "she was associated with and sympathetic to leftist movement," and led a local committee to defend Communist leader Claudia Jones.[2]

First elected Multnomah County Circuit Court Judge in 1972, she was re-elected to four consecutive six-year terms. A year after arriving in Portland in 1948 with a child and $12, she married former Tuskegee Airman CARL DEIZ D6. They lived at **9340 N. Portsmouth Avenue**.

 ## 2 Portland's Alternative Newspapers

The old brick building at **1714 NW Overton Street** (formerly a Wells Fargo stable) was the home of the **Portland Reporter**. This daily newspaper was established in 1959 by journalists on strike against *The Oregonian* and the *Oregon Journal* and was published by Portland labor unions until 1964. The publishers tried to break the strike by importing scabs from outside Oregon, mainly from the South, and succeeded when too many journalists surrendered and crossed picket lines. Despite the struggle of Portland unions, the way was cleared for the current monopoly of New York's Newhouse chain. Newhouse had bought *The Oregonian* in 1950 and paid $8 million for the *Journal* during the strike in 1961 only to abandon it in 1982 (the chain added the *Portland Business Journal* in 1995). In recent years, however, alternative papers such as **The Portland Alliance**, **Willamette Week** and its predecessors, and even the relatively conservative *Portland Tribune* have sprung up as occasional gadflies to *The Oregonian*. One consequence of its out-of-state-ownership and monopoly position is that *The Oregonian's* former slogan, "If it matters to Oregonians, it's in *The Oregonian*," has often suffered well-deserved ridicule when scooped on major local stories, including scandals of politicians such as Senator Robert Packwood, big businesses such as Portland General Electric, and corrupt government institutions such as the Portland Police Red Squad F26.

 **Bernard Jolles**

In 1963, the Oregon State Bar denied admission to **Bernard Jolles** on the grounds that he failed to meet its moral standards by having belonged to the Communist Party. In 1956, Jolles had moved to Portland from New York, where he had been a longshoreman, and later graduated from the Northwest College of Law (now Lewis & Clark Law School) with top honors. After several appeals, the Oregon Supreme Court ordered his admission and Attorney Jolles was finally able to practice his profession. He practiced law so well, in fact, that in 1988, he was elected president of the Oregon State Bar. His office is at ***721 SW Oak Street***.

Earlier, the Bar also denied admission to Frank V. Patterson, another Northwest College of Law graduate, because he refused to cooperate with the House Un-American Activities Committee **(HUAC)** D32 when it held hearings in Portland in 1954. Patterson was also eventually admitted.

 **Frederick L. Schuman**

In July 1963, over a year before the infamous Tonkin Gulf Resolution, Portland State College (which became Portland State University in 1969) visiting political science professor **Frederick L. Schuman** (later a regular member of the faculty) made what was arguably the first speech in Oregon against U.S. military intervention by President John F. Kennedy in the then little-noticed Vietnamese Civil War.

Students for a Democratic Society (SDS)

SDS was first organized in Portland in 1964 in a house at **6008 SE 55th Avenue** at Woodstock Boulevard. Led by Reedies Jeremy Brecher, Phil Wikelund, and Mike Athag, it focused on college students and antiwar and draft actions. One of their recruits at a fundraising party for the *Portland Reporter* was the future "Marxist environmentalist" Mike Davis. Future historian of the Left Maurice Isserman joined several years later when he came to Reed.

 Subversive Actvities Control Board (SACB) 1964

In contrast to the low-key opposition Portlanders expressed to HUAC D32 ten years earlier, they found their voice when another relic of the McCarthy Era, the **Subversive Activities Control Board (SACB)** came to town in 1964 (former Portland Mayor Dorothy Mc-Coullugh Lee, who received advice from the RED SQUAD F26 was appointed to the SACB by President Eisenhower and served until 1962). Hundreds of protesters surrounded the same U.S. courthouse used by HUAC in 1954, and over a hundred Portland area college faculty and staff signed their names to a large protest ad in *The Oregonian.* The board was established under the McCarran Internal Security Act of 1950 and required persons it designated as Communists to register as such—making them subject to arrest and deportation to concentration camps (also authorized under the legislation) in the event of a national emergency.

Like HUAC, the SACB relied on paid informers to identify its targets. In 1964 in Portland, that informer was David Reilly, whom the FBI paid to join the Communist Party in 1958. He named two Portlanders, retired carpenter Norman Haaland and Navy veteran Ben Jacobson, who were defended by attorney Nels Peterson. In 1968, the U.S. Supreme Court ruled the registration provisions of the McCarran Act unconstitutional.

 Allen Ginsberg

Poet **Allen Ginsberg** lived in Portland in Mrs. Alice Strong's garden cottage at **2525 SW Montgomery** for several months in the 1960s. His appearance at PSU in 1967 caused the student paper to be shut down by PSU president Bradford Millard for publishing a nude photo of the poet. His attendance at a Beatles concert at the Memorial Coliseum in August of 1964 inspired a poem, "Portland Coliseum," in which he describes it as the "New World Auditorium" filled with a "red sweatered ecstasy" contained by a police line.[3]

 Russell Krueger

One of HUAC's final efforts to suppress Portland's Left came in 1967, when **Russell Krueger**, among the last of the McCarthy Era's local corps of paid informers, testified in Washington, D. C., about his undercover role for the FBI at PSU and Reed College. Krueger said he joined the Communist Party in December 1963 and reported to the FBI until October 1964. Like former Reed student Homer Owen who named fellow students before HUAC D32 in 1954, Krueger accused about twenty-five PSU and Reed students of having belonged to party youth clubs at the colleges and one "downtown," but only Joe Uris, Denise Jacobson, James Berland, and John Van Hyning were named in the press reports of the hearings. He also named many others as members of the Fair Play for Cuba Committee, Reed College and PSU Students for Peace and Students for Civil Liberties, the W. E. B. Du Bois Club, the FOCUS Club at Reed (later the Political Affairs Club), and the Helsinki Youth Festival Committee. Photos taken of Portland demonstrations—most likely taken by the Portland Police RED SQUAD F26—constitute a useful list of historic sites associated with local peace and civil rights efforts. But at the HUAC hearing they were used to identify those Krueger named as Communists and radicals. Photos introduced in evidence included demonstrations at Reed College in 1961, on Hiroshima Day 1962, for civil rights on June 23, 1963,

E: 1960–1973
Peaceniks & Civil Rights

July 3, 1964, and September 28, 1964, against **SACB** E6 in
April 1964 and January 1965, against the Vietnam War
at the Pioneer Post Office on February 20 and 27, 1965,
and at the International Days of Protest on October 16,
1965. Donald Hamerquist, openly describing himself as
an organizer for the Oregon Communist Party, said he
"always thought Krueger was too clumsy and obvious to
be an FBI informer."[4]

HUAC had become so notorious by 1969 that it
changed its name to the "House Internal Security Committee." It was finally abolished in 1976.

 Civil Rights Protests

Portland's black community experienced several serious
street protests between 1967 and 1969. In June 1969, at
least twenty fires were started along former NE Union
Avenue (now MLK Boulevard). The formerly busy business district never recovered, and some lots remain vacant more than thirty-five years later. A Portland police
officer, then in his 20s, remembers "standing at what was
then **NE Union and Fremont Street**. Every building in
my line of sight was on fire. There were people in the
streets. I heard occasional gunfire." The Portland Police
Department was accused of overreacting and that officer, now Portland Mayor Tom Potter, admits the police
department was not prepared. "We went out there with
very little training, very little equipment and a huge gulf
between us and the African American community."[5]
That gulf had not narrowed sufficiently by 1981 to
prevent a racist outburst by white police. Officers Craig
Ward and Jim Galloway tossed four dead possums in
front of the Burger Barn, a black-owned restaurant in
Northeast Portland, and found support from hundreds
of their fellow officers who marched on city hall in a
successful protest to reverse their dismissal.

An even more outrageous racist police act occurred in
1985 when white officers Gary Barbour and Bruce Pantley killed Lloyd Stevenson, a black Fred Meyer security
guard who had tried to cool a shoplifting confrontation in a Northeast 7-Eleven store. When Greg Cavic, a

white man, began an argument with Stevenson, Barbour, backed by Pantley, applied a "sleeper hold," choking and killing Stevenson. On the day of Stevenson's funeral, two more white officers, Richard Montee and Paul Wikersham added insult to injury. In the parking lot of the East Precinct, they sold about thirty T-shirts declaring, "Don't Choke 'Em, Smoke 'Em" to fellow officers. As in the infamous possum incident, none of the racist officers were punished despite large-scale public demonstrations. Mayor Bud Clark's effort to fire Montee and Wikersham was reversed and although a public inquest panel found Barbour and Pantley guilty of criminally negligent homicide, no grand jury would indict them. Barbour remained on the force as late as 1999.

 Black Panther Party

The long history of such racism among the Portland police was one reason the Portland chapter of the **Black Panther Party** was organized on the principle of self-defense and a revolutionary ideology. These characteristics disguised it from traditional civil rights organizations that sought racial equality under capitalism and believed that police behavior could be "reformed" with the hiring of more black officers. The BPP operated the Fred Hampton Peoples Health Clinic at 109 N. Russell Street (named to honor the party leader murdered in his bed by Chicago police in one of the FBI's notorious Counter Intelligence Program (CONTELPRO) from 1969 to 1978. They also offered the George Jackson Memorial Free Breakfast program (named for another party leader killed trying to escape from prison) at the Highland United Church of Christ at *4635 NE 9th Avenue* in 1969 and a free dental clinic at *2341 N. Williams Avenue* in the late 1960s. When Portland police shot and wounded Albert Williams at the 3819 NE Union Avenue office of the Black Panthers in 1970, his lawyer, Nick Chaivoe, told a protest rally of hundreds in downtown Portland that the police shot without justification. Kent Ford was a Black Panther leader who lived at *23 NE San Rafael Street*.

E: 1960–1973
Peaceniks & Civil Rights

Charles CX Debiew

A black Muslim minister, **Charles CX Debiew**, and his wife, Sister Iantha, opened the Temple of Islam in their home at 4056 N. Williams Avenue in the early 1960s. In 1969, a more successful Mohammed's Mosque 62 was established at **707 NE Fremont Street**, together with a school, a bean pie bakery, a café, and a fish market.

 Ho Chi Minh Trail

A path that skirts the freeway from Goose Hollow toward PSU was jokingly dubbed the **"Ho Chi Minh Trail"** by local antiwar and counter-culture activists in the late 1960s.

 The Flogger

At the corner of **NW 25th Avenue and Vaughn Street** is a rare tribute to the American working class: **"The Flogger,"** sculptor Frederick Lippman's vision of a man swinging a sledgehammer. It was commissioned in 1969 by Ernest Swigert's steel mill and stands on its property.

 Walter Priestly

Walter Priestly, an avowed Socialist representing the Ainsworth Park area of Northeast Portland, served in the state legislature from the late 1960s through the 1970s. Some of his political protests were especially dramatic. He jumped off the **Broadway Bridge** as part of the "Inner-Tube Navy" to protest warships coming for the Rose Festival and was arrested in Vancouver at the "White Train" protest against nuclear weapons transport. In the 1970s, radical attorney DON CHAMBERS F11 was his administrative assistant in the state legislature.

 Battle of the Park Blocks

In early May 1970, President Richard Nixon ordered U.S. troops to expand the Vietnam War by publicly invading neighboring Cambodia. Spontaneous protests broke out all over the nation, during which four students were killed by National Guard troops at Kent State University in Ohio and two by police at Jackson State University in Mississippi. In Portland on May 6, PSU students and faculty experienced the most powerful local event in the national outrage: hundreds went out on strike and the campus was closed for four days.

Gathering in the Park Blocks, demonstrators persuaded many other students and faculty to support the strike, and showed their outrage by blocking traffic with barricades built from park benches and debris from nearby construction sites.

On orders from Oregon Governor Tom McCall, PSU president Greg Wolfe reopened the university May 11. But when protesters refused a police order to take down a first aid tent, police dressed in riot gear attacked them in wedge formation with clubs. Almost thirty protesters were injured seriously enough to be hospitalized in what became known as the **Battle of the Park Blocks**. More than five thousand Portlanders marched on city hall to demand the organizers of the police riot—City Commissioner Francis Ivancie and Police Chief Donald McNamara—be punished.

Years later, informed judgments of the event differ. Strike historian Dory Hylton noted there was plenty to protest against: the re-escalation and expansion of the Vietnam War, the shooting deaths of the Kent State and Jackson State students, the imprisonment of Black Panther Bobby Seale, and the shipment of nerve gas into Oregon. Hylton believes "the students were absolutely, 100 percent committed to non-violence."[6]

But PSU history professor David A. Horowitz, who supported the antiwar demonstration at the time, had second thoughts, suggesting that tactics such as the blocking of traffic and disrupting classes may have alienated the public. "If you're trying to change society for the better," he argued, "you have to have respect for the people you're trying to enroll in the changes, or you may end up marginalized."[7]

Strike leader Doug Weiskopf, on the other hand, looks back without regrets. "I can't think of anything

I'd [have] done differently," he says, "I was trying to make a point as loudly as I could and dramatically as I could. We got the message out, we made our point, and we made it pretty much violence- or vandalism-free."[8] And, referring to Horowitz as well as similar comments by Joe Uris, another student leader, Weiskopf laments, "What has made these tigers of the past suddenly wimp out and start whining about how we were wrong to be 'so angry' and to disturb the delicate sensibilities of an American public who would rather have ignored the horrors of the daily slaughter in Southeast Asia?"[9]

The People's Army Jamboree & Vortex I

The People's Army Jamboree was organized in the wake of the May BATTLE OF THE PARK BLOCKS E15 to counter an expected appearance by President Nixon at the August 1970 American Legion convention in Portland. But influential Portlanders worried about the potential for violence persuaded Governor Tom McCall and enough of its antiwar organizers to divert its potential protestors to a state-sponsored "little Woodstock" called **Vortex I** that was outside Portland in Clackamas County and featured rock music. In hindsight, some observed that the event showed the ability of political leaders to significantly reduce an antiwar protest by tempting insufficiently ideological young people from political action by simply offering them a law enforcement-free good time.[10] Years later, it was revealed that the Portland Police RED SQUAD F26 had violated the rights of the original organizers with infiltration, wiretaps, and both secret and aggressively "in-your-face" surveillance. They also urged Portland newspaper publishers and station managers to slant their coverage against the protests by assigning only unsympathetic reporters and editors.[11]

1970s Hipsters

Hipster protestors with a literary bent hung out at Reuben's 5 Peace and Pizza Tavern at **1239 SW Jefferson** in the early 1970s. Among the regulars were Mike

McCusker, John Bertels, Art Honeyman, Wally Chambers, and Walt Curtis.

 ## Northwest Liberation Front (NLF)

One radical group that emerged from the New Left was the **Northwest Liberation Front (NLF)**, which the Portland Police RED SQUAD F26 claims was linked to the Weather Underground. Named for the line from Bob Dylan's 1965 "Subterranean Homesick Blues," "You don't need a weatherman/To know which way the wind blows," the weathermen (and women) (who changed their names when they went underground), were originally a faction within the SDS E5 that accepted violence as a political tactic while rejecting "white skin privilege" in an effort to support those they considered to be their allies, such as the BPP E10. The local NLF may have been responsible for blowing up a replica of the Liberty Bell outside city hall in November 1970 an act intended to recall the May "police riot" in the PARK BLOCKS E15.

Weather Underground leaders Karen Lee Latimer and Jeff Jones were identified as operating underground in Oregon, and several others surrendered from hiding (and went to jail) in Portland, as did Katherine Ann Power in Lebanon in 1993. Weatherman Trim Bissell was arrested in Eugene in 1987 after hiding for seventeen years. After serving time in federal prison, he returned to Eugene and died there in 2002. Later, some activists motivated by the radical environmentalist ideology of the Earth Liberation Front were charged with arson against the property of twenty-first century lumber barons and other designated commercial enemies in Oregon.

There was an unsuccessful kidnapping of wealthy Portlander Ira Keller (of Keller Fountain and Keller Auditorium fame), who led the destruction of South Portland's Jewish and Italian neighborhoods in the name of "urban renewal," a robbery of a gunshop, and the Country Kitchen restaurant. The most violent act in Portland against the Vietnam War came when military recruiting centers at **4008 NE Union Avenue** (now MLK Blvd) on January 2 and at **5030 SE Foster Road** on January 4, 1973, were damaged by bombs, an action intended to protest the U.S. bombing of a children's hospital in Hanoi, Vietnam. Several antiwar activists including PSU professor Frank Giese, who was fired by the PSU president after his indictment despite faculty protests, were convicted of conspiracy in connection with the bombings and served prison time. Memorial services for Giese (1916–2006) were held at River View Cemetery, 8421 SW Macadam Avenue.

According to Lynn Meyer, Giese "was one of his comrades in the NLF." The others included Susan Stoner, James Cronin, James Akers, Robert McSherry, Leslie McKeel, Max Severin, and Chester Wallace.[12]

1960–1973 Notes

1. *Willamette Week*, June 9, 1999.

2. Intelligence Division Report, Portland Bureau of Police, August 15, 1960. Charley Trimble to Chief Hillbruner. "Confidential Information, Subject: Deiz, Mercedes."

3. Reprinted from Mikal Gilmore, "And the Bank Played On," *New York Times*, August 24, 2005.

4. "Oregon Communist Leader Admits Inducting Informant," *Oregon Journal*, April 15, 1967.

5. "Potter on Riots, Redevelopments," *The Oregonian*, June 15, 2006.

6. "Four Days that Changed Portland," *Vanguard*, May 5, 2005.

7. Endnote 6.

8. Endnote 6.

9. "Years Later, Questions Unanswered," *Vanguard*, May 7, 2005.

10. Matt Love, *The Far Out Story of Vortex I*, (Pacific City, OR: Nestucca Spit Press, 2004).

11. Portland Bureau of Police Intelligence Report, February 10, 1972, from officer C. F. Trimble to Lt. Melvin Hulett, "Intelligence Planning, Functions and Critique of American Legion and People's Army Jamboree Activities."

12 http://www.livelogcity.com/users/copkiller11/434.html.

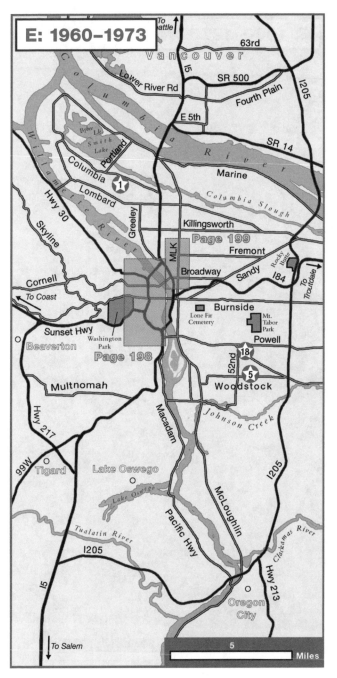

E: 1960–1973

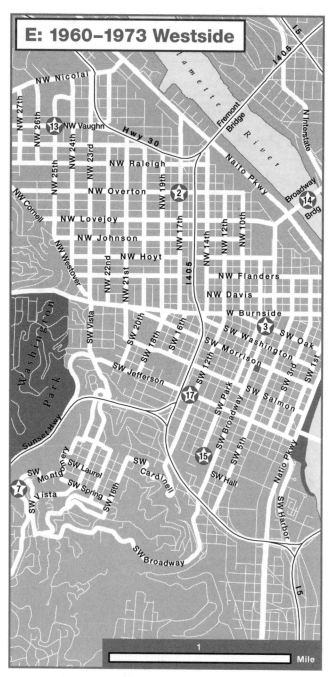

E: 1960–1973 Westside

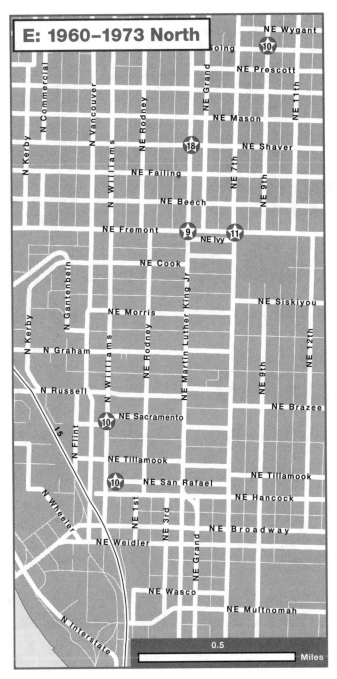

E: 1960–1973 North

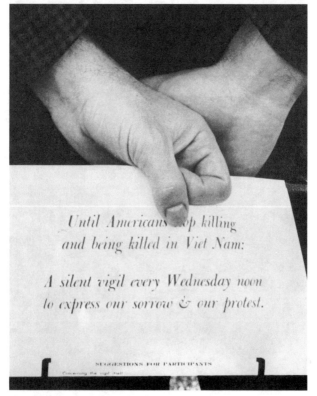

Until Americans *top killing*
and being killed in Viet Nam:

A silent vigil every Wednesday noon
to express our sorrow & our protest.

SUGGESTIONS FOR PARTICIPANTS

Concerning the vigil itself

In the Park Blocks, sixty students kept a weekly peace vigil in the late 1960s. These images come from the PSU yearbook from 1967. *The Viking 1967.*

 Joe Uris, shown in a photo from the 1967 Portland State University yearbook, was one of twenty-five students from the area named by Russell Krueger at HUAC hearings in Washington, D.C. *The Viking 1967.*

 Portland's black community protested the expansion of Emanuel Hospital into the heart of their community. Frustration over being forced to continually make way for Portland's "progress" fueled these protests. *Oregon Historical Society, CN023743.*

 Above: A political rally on August 30, 1967, turned into two nights of rioting in the Irvington neighborhood. Two to three hundred people caused tens of thousands of dollars in damage. *Oregon Historical Society, OrHi25045.* Right: The Emanuel protests from Icky A. *Icky A.*

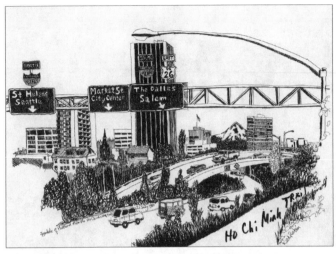

 This Rick Rubin drawing is from a 1982 calendar. It shows the Ho Chi Minh Trail leading towards the Portland city center. *Rick Rubin*.

 The Flogger, an artistic tribute to the working classes by sculptor Frederick Lippman, stands on the corner of NW 25th Avenue and Vaughn Street. *Michael Munk*.

 Walter Priestly represented the Northeast Ainsworth Park area of Portland in the state legislature from the late 1960s through the 1970s as a Socialist. *Priscilla Carrasco.*

Walter Priestly and Mary Jane Brewster at an August 6, 1966, peace walk. Protestors walked from Portland to Salem on Highway 99E. *City of Portland Archives, A2004-005.*

Scenes like this were common during the Vietnam-era protests in Portland. Clay Axelrod is being arrested here in 1967. *Oregon Historical Society, CN001484.*

 PSU students went on strike May 6, 1970, to protest the killing of Kent State and Jackson State students by the National Guard and police. The campus was closed for four days. *The Viking 1970.*

 In 1969, this peace march wound through downtown Portland, with tens of thousands participating. *Oregon Historical Society, OrHi23934.*

 Hundreds of students walked out of classes during the PSU strike. *The Viking 1970.*

 While students were on strike, they made signs at the University. *The Viking 1970.*

When Governor Tom McCall ordered PSU open on May 11, 1970, protestors refused to take down a first aid tent in the Park Blocks. The police, dressed in riot gear, attacked the protestors with clubs, and over thirty people were injured in what became known as the Battle of the Park Blocks. *The Viking 1970.*

 The People's Army Jamboree, a protest group organized to counter an expected appearance by President Richard Nixon in Portland, was under heavy surveillance by the Red Squad F26. Ronald Betts was photographed at an August 31, 1970, rally. *City of Portland Archives, A2004-005.*

Frank Giese, a PSU professor, was convicted and served prison time for his connection with the NLF. He's shown here, in the center, marching with his wife, Jane, in a July 18, 1966, peace march. *City of Portland Archives, A2004-005.*

Taken in 1970 at a peace rally, this photo shows a member of the Women's Auxiliary of the ILWU wearing a coat signed by the ILWU's Members for Peace. *Oregon Historical Society, OrHi104358.*

In 2002, protesters marched down SW Broadway Avenue to the Hilton Hotel where President George W. Bush was staying. When the Portland Police set up a roadblock, they went straight through it. *Bette Lee.*

F: 1974–Present
Identities & Environment

Recent decades have seen a significant shift in the ideology of dissent in America that has been reflected in Portland. The suppression of radical political parties during the Cold War and the McCarthy Era has been both the cause and the effect of the rise of identity politics—those movements for equality and justice for race, gender, sexual preference, and national or ethnic groups—as well as organizations devoted to separate issues such as peace, globalization, animal rights, and the environment. But many of the recent movements have radical roots: the **1948 Progressive Party D25** welcomed the support of "Bachelors for Wallace," which became the base for an early gay-rights group, the Mattachine Society. The women's liberation movement developed from the experiences of women in New Left groups during the 1960s. But with the exception of a revived anarchist movement, most twenty-first century dissenters do not locate the source of their complaints within the nature of capitalism, so they do not consider a radical reorganization of society necessary to reach their goals. To the extent that they hope to achieve their objectives through reforms within capitalism, they distinguish themselves from previous radical history even if they practice or contemplate militant, confrontational, or even violent tactics. The strategy that guided most radical groups through much of the twentieth century—the organization of a popular political movement or party devoted to replacing capitalism with Socialism—has, except for a modest rival of anarchism, given way to the goal of reform through interest group pressure on existing political and economic organizations and structures.

A compilation of forty-five street protests in Portland during the 1990s shows that the leading subjects were labor (including globalization) for seventeen, foreign policy for twelve, identity/civil rights for eight, and environment (mainly forest) for seven.[1]

Since the United States's defeat by the Vietnamese and the decline in the New Left, several institutions were established in Portland to provide these developing protest groups with a voice and alternatives to mainstream media—just like FIREBRAND A5 described itself in 1895. These include the community radio station KBOO and the progressive monthly *The Portland Alliance*. Michael Wells, founded the counter-culture *Portland Scribe,* which was once published at the CENTENARY WILBUR METHODIST CHURCH F2, and its predecessor *Willamette Bridge*. He later joined the less controversial "metrosexual" entertainment and cultural weekly, *Willamette Week*. The Red and Black Café at 2139 SE Division Street also makes radicals and protestors especially welcome.

Protest movements have always been associated with their bookstores and the movements of this period were no exception. Bookstores serving activists have included The Days & Nights Bookstore on SW Broadway, across from Portland State University, operated by Jean-Paul Pickens, an organizer for the Socialist Party's Young People's Socialist League; Radical Education Project's United Front Bookstore founded by Frank Giese; the Community Party's JOHN REED BOOKSTORE F13 on SE Hawthorne Boulevard; and, most recently, the collectively-run Laughing Horse Books at 12 NE 10th Avenue just off E. Burnside Street (which mirrors the location of a better-known competitor, Powell's City of Books, at NW 10th Avenue and Burnside Street). The revived Wobblies and anarchists, who provide militance and noisy energy at Portland demonstrations, have a bookstore in the basement of the Liberty Hall at 311 N. Ivy.

Other activist institutions in Portland in the early twenty-first century include the CENTENARY WILBUR METHODIST CHURCH F2, which hosted almost every organization of dissenters from the 1950s to 1980. Red Rose School provided movement-based education at the Friends Meeting House, 4312 SE Stark Street, until it closed in 2002. Koinonia House, on the PSU campus at 633 SW

Montgomery Street, was a center for meetings, memorials, and services. The Sisters of the Road café at 133 NW 6th Avenue was founded on the Catholic Worker Movement philosophy of Peter Maurin and Dorothy Day. The Pacific Green Party, originally a voice of the environmental movement, has contested some local elections and usually causes debate when third party candidates such as Ralph Nader, who drew fifty thousand votes in Oregon in the 2000 Presidential election, run under its banner. But the Internet has probably become the most significant mode of communication and source of dissenting news on the Left. Widely available blogs and websites, such as the Portland Independent Media Center at http://portland.indymedia.org, are a growing alternative to mainstream media.

As this final section of the guide is devoted to more recent people and events—some of which readers may have witnessed or even participated in—the historical distance from the sites diminishes and their meaning may become more personal. So as some entries can be associated with personal memories rather than what we read or see in photos, documentary films, and videos, we become aware of the present as history. What we witness today is history tomorrow.

 1 Portland Gay Liberation Front

Less than a year after the Stonewall Rebellion of New York gays, the **Portland Gay Liberation Front** was organized on March 10, 1970, at the CENTENARY WILBUR METHODIST CHURCH F2 by Holly Hart and Jack Wilkinson, who were both twenty-two years old.[2] Five years earlier, the city had forced Portland's premier gay bar, The Harbor Club at **736 SW 1st Avenue** (now Paddy's Bar and Grill), to close.[3] Frank Ivancie, the last of Portland's old-line mayors, who held office from 1980–1984, led the resistance to gays and lesbians in city government. "No homos in fire houses," was one of his more notorious declarations.

② Centenary Wilbur Methodist Church

Recalling the record of the Methodist Federation for Social Action D37 in the 1950s and 1960s, is there something about the Methodist church in Portland that recommends it to radicals? Indeed, as early as the 1950s the Federation already had sponsored a talk by then GOP Senator Wayne Morse in the **Centenary Wilbur Methodist Church** at *215 SE 9th Avenue*. By 1970, the church had been transformed from a prosperous middle-class institution reflecting its early neighborhood demographics of the nineteenth century to the end of World War II into a counter-culture center that served Portland dissidents and hippies. The historic church itself never recovered from damage caused by the Columbus Day storm of 1962, but its education building survived. Until the church's demise in 1980, it welcomed dissident groups ranging from the Gay Liberation Front and the People's Liberation Army to the New American Movement, the Poor People's Alliance, and the Trojan Decommissioning Alliance, bringing down surveillance by the Portland Red Squad F26.[4] Many Portlanders associate the church with the site's later tenants, the music venue La Luna and the Pine Street Theater. In 2006, the building was remodeled into the Pine Street Lofts.

③ City Club of Portland

Although its male members rejected women in three consecutive elections, the **City Club of Portland**, which usually holds its meeting in the Governor Hotel at *614 SW 11th Avenue*, finally accepted them in 1973 with a 65 percent majority vote. The Multnomah Club also allowed women to vote in the 1970s. They were still well ahead of the other men-only clubs that dominated Portland's business and political life during the twentieth century. The University Club did not admit women until 1990 and the Arlington Club, whose members meet at *811 SW Salmon Street*, hung on until 1991. During the struggle over women at the Arlington in 1990, *The*

Oregonian published by Arlington Club member Fred Stickel, killed a story reporting the Club's efforts to delay a vote on a city ordinance that would required them to let women into the Club.[5]

 Portland Labor College

The second coming of the **Portland Labor College** B32 occurred in 1977, when several unions and other sponsors, led by the former International Woodworkers of America (IWA), opened a center for labor education under the direction of Norman Diamond. Before closing in 1984, the college, located in the former Operating Engineers Union Hall on SW 2nd Avenue, also sponsored a theater troupe that revived the former name of the Portland Labor Players, which performed plays about the working class struggle, such as *Season of Silence: Life and Labor in the Oregon City Woolen Mills*, a play about historic attacks on Chinese workers. Plays were outdoors at INTERNATIONAL LONGSHORE AND WAREHOUSE UNION'S (ILWU) BLOODY THURSDAY C9 observances in Oaks Park and all around town at, for example, the Musicians Union Hall at *325 NE 20th Avenue*, St. Johns YMCA, 8010 N. Charleston Avenue, and the Theater Workshop, *511 SE 60th Avenue*.

 Bill Walton

Bill Walton, counter-culture center for the NBA Champion Portland Trailblazers in 1977, shared a November 5 birthday with Eugene Debs and lived at *2337 NW Kearney Street*. The police RED SQUAD F26 accused him of joining anti-Vietnam War protests while in college and, in Portland, of associating with radicals, including Jack Scott, a sports journalist working to develop political consciences of professional athletes. Walton visited his old place twenty years later and noted "it hadn't changed at all"—although the rent, then $65 a month, surely had.

F: 1974–Present
Identities & Protests

Portland's **Francis J. Murnane Wharf** at the seawall at the foot of *SW Ankeny Street* is the only public memorial to a union leader in the state of Oregon, a fact that testifies to the pro-business, anti-labor bias of official history. The floating dock, dedicated by ILWU C9 President Harry Bridges in 1979, honors the late leader of the Congress of Industrial Organization's (CIO) International Woodworkers of America and later of ILWU Local 8 who died in 1968 while conducting a union meeting. During the McCarthy Era, Murnane defended radicals as secretary of the Julia Eaton Ruuttila Defense Committee in 1948 and, as head of the Harry Bridges Defense Committee in 1949, he denounced the RED SQUAD F26 for making Bridges a special target. He was also a PROGRESSIVE PARTY D25 candidate for the state legislature in 1948 and in his later years became of leader of historic preservation efforts in Portland. Murnane believed that radicals "[Eugene] Debs and [Bill] Haywood showed the way" for unions. Bridges noted at the dedication that Murnane always hoped "that the old slogan of the Wobblies would come true: 'Workers of the World Unite.'" Father Bertram Griffin of St. Andrews Catholic Church blessed the wharf for the use of "radicals, labor activists, and lovers." Among the major supporters of the memorial was his fellow ILWU leader, the late JESSE STRANAHAN F9.[6]

7 Richard Ross

Although McCarthyism was considered by many to be dead, its hidden secrets continue to be revealed. Longtime Portland KGW-TV news anchor **Richard Ross** (later at KATU) waited until 1977 to confess he had been a FBI informer in the 1950s, reporting on the politics of his colleagues in Portland's TV, radio, and print journalism. Ross retired from KATU in 1986 and took a public relations job promoting the Oregon Lottery.

8 Stew Albert

Portlander **Stew Albert** (1939–2006) was one of the "leaders" of the yippies in the 1960s, and an unindicted co-conspirator of the "Chicago 7" defendants whose convictions for organizing violence at the 1968 Democratic convention in Chicago were reversed on appeal. In 1985, he moved to Portland where he remained an activist and produced his popular website. One of his local political observations was that most speakers at Portland antiwar demonstrations were boring, and he argued for adoption of yippie tactics such as spontaneous self-expression and a fun spirit to liven them up. He is buried in the Havurah cemetery, *5656 SW Humphrey Boulevard*.

9 Jesse & Lois Stranahan

Jesse and Lois Stranahan were active in almost every local political and labor struggle from the time they arrived in Portland after meeting at Commonwealth College in Mena, Arkansas, in the late 1930s. Jesse was a journalist on the CIO's newspaper the *Labor New Dealer* and a leader in the ILWU's Clerks Local 40. Lois remains an activist in labor politics. One of her arrests, for gathering petition signatures against the sales tax at the Fred Meyer store at *SE 82nd Avenue and Foster Road*, occurred in 1989. Years later, a jury awarded her more than $2 million for the false arrest, but the Oregon Supreme Court reversed that decision.

10 Julia Ruuttila

Julia Ruuttila—also known by her maiden name Godman, previous married names Bertram and Eaton, and pen names Kathleen Cronin and Kathleen Ruuttila—was prominent among the Old Left radicals for whom age alone put an end to their activism.[7] In her lifetime (1907–1991) there were few labor or civil liberties struggles in which Ruuttila did not participate, especially those conducted by the CIO Woodworkers and ILWU unions. She was both victim and militant opponent of McCarthyism. She participated in anti-Vietnam War protests, fought against Oregon nerve gas storage and the sales tax, and worked for public power. In the 1930s, she organized the effort to free the last of the CENTRALIA WOBBLIES B27, and in 1948 she provided help for the VANPORT FLOOD VICTIMS D21. Ruuttila was fired by the Oregon Public Welfare Commission for her support of the Vanport refugees when S. Eugene Allen, editor of the *Oregon Labor Press*, denounced her as "another energetic little lady who promotes the Communist Party line." In turn, Ruuttila described Allen as "the most vicious right wing." Frequently depicted in the press as a dissenter, Ruuttila, then 66, together with MARTINA GANGLE CURL F13, 68, was jailed in 1973 for refusing to leave offices at **SW Broadway and Morrison Street** to protest rising utility. In one of her poems, she counted the carriage rings in Northwest Portland curbs and found more on afflu-ent blocks than poor ones. "Carriage rings," her poem concludes, "defined the social status/In old Portland."

 **11** Don Chambers

> Old revolutionaries are the gentle dignity of a city.
> —Rick Rubin on Don Chambers, 1985

The Oregon Supreme Court upheld the two-year sus-pension of attorney **Don Chambers** in 1982, although, because he was almost blind and unable to walk, he had already retired a year earlier. Chambers, of an anarchist bent, was called "the most radical lawyer in Portland" for his defense, with fees, of "the poor, the Communists, Trotskyites, Chicanos, Native Americans, and prostitutes" as well as motorcycle gang members and students ar-rested in the 1970 BATTLE OF THE PARK BLOCKS E15. With a tiny office next to his Check Store locker service on **NW 2nd Avenue and Burnside Street**, Chambers was the subject of many complaints from more elevated mem-bers of the Bar, although the revival of a local chapter of the National Lawyers Guild made defense of unpopular causes more respectable.

 **Benjamin Linder**

Benjamin Linder (1960–1987) is commemorated with a bench ("a bench against forgetting," his sister called it) and a tree in Wallace Park at *NW 25th Avenue and Raleigh Street*, near his former home, where four hundred people marked the tenth anniversary of his death.[8] Linder was assassinated by U.S.-state-sponsored terrorists in 1987 while building water projects in Nicaragua for the benefit of poor rural residents. A professional clown and engineering graduate of Oregon State University, Linder volunteered his services to the Sandinista government, which the Reagan administration sought to overthrow by funding the counter-revolutionary Contras. He is also remembered by the Ben Linder Construction Brigade. The seventh contingent of its volunteers went to Corinto, Nicaragua (one of Portland's sister cities), in 1996 to work on local projects in Linder's honor.

One Linder Brigade member was the late **Dr. David Hanson "Punch" Worthington** (1935–2006), a longtime labor, peace, and health activist from Keizer, Oregon. His family asked that "Punch would be best honored if well-wishers voted for leaders who will defend our bill of rights, preserve our wilderness, fight for socialized health care, and protect the rights of labor unions in the U.S. and abroad."

 Hank & Martina Gangle Curl

Veteran Communist Party members **Hank and Martina Gangle Curl** were among the proprietors of the John Reed Bookstore at *4700 SE Hawthorne Boulevard* and offered Portlanders leftist books and literature until it closed in 1993.

Hank Curl, who was born in 1913, lives in their home at *2237 NE Clackamas Street*, which has been occupied by important Portland artists for many years. It was originally owned by Harry Wentz, dean of the Portland Museum Art School, and later by his friends, the outstanding Northwest radical painters, brothers Arthur and

Albert Runquist. Their Works Progress Administration (WPA) murals can be seen at the University of Oregon Library, Pendleton High School, and the Sedro Wooley, Washington, Post Office. Martina Curl's Rose City Park School mural at **2334 NE 57th Avenue** features the early white migration to Oregon. Efforts to save her artwork if the school is closed have been planned.

Pete Seeger

In 1996, radical folksinger **Pete Seeger's** last Portland concert—a benefit for the Northwest Tree Planters and Farm Workers United (PCUN)—was held at Benson High School at **546 NE 12th Avenue**. In 1955, students made a bootleg recording of his concert at Reed College, but he immediately demanded they stop selling the double ten-inch LP set.

Celebration of John Reed's Birth

On October 22, 1987, Pioneer Square was the scene of a celebration of John Reed's birth. A small group of local writers, including David Milholland, the late Fred DeWolfe, Brian Booth, and David Horowitz, with financial support from Reed fan Corliss Lamont in New York, held an appreciative reading of his writing. The organizers later established the Oregon Cultural Heritage Commission, which installed the REED MEMORIAL BENCH IN WASHINGTON PARK B20.

May Day in Portland

May Day observances in Portland have been revived in recent years with marches downtown supported by a few unions and younger radicals. The police attack on demonstrators in 2001 exposed the role of rightist police and the RED SQUAD F26. Black clad anarchists lent energy to the marches up Broadway and downtown with drum corps, while cheerleaders roused spirits with well-coordinated protest yells.

17 Portland's Halls

In the 1990s **Finnish Hall** was moved from its original location at 3425 N. Montana Avenue and remodeled into a Community Center for Kaiser Permanente's N. Interstate Avenue complex. It was one of the old Portland ethnic and nationality halls that radicals seemed to favor for their meetings and social gatherings since early in the twentieth century. In addition to Finnish Hall were **Norse Hall** at *111 NE 11th Avenue*, **Linnea Hall** at *2066 NW Irving Street*, **Italian Federation Hall** at *SW 4th Avenue and Madison Street*, **Swiss Hall** at *SW 3rd Avenue and Jefferson Street*, **Hibernian Hall** on NE Russell Street, and **Turn Verein Hall**, which stood at *SW 4th Ave and Yamhill Street*.

18 Little Beirut

The story of how Portland achieved the national nickname of **Little Beirut** has been traced to former **President George H. W. Bush**, who denied coining the name. After several smaller demonstrations against him, Bush was evidently shocked when fifteen thousand marched up Broadway on January 12, 1991, in the first major demonstration against his imminent invasion of Iraq.

His son **George W. Bush** also has not been warmly received in Portland. In 2002, police rioted with tear gas and rubber bullets against thousands of demonstrators while Bush was raising money for Oregon Republican Senator Gordon Smith at the Hilton Hotel downtown. The next year, five thousand protested another Bush fundraiser at the University of Portland. During the 2004 election campaign, Bush avoided the city, retreating to the suburbs with an indoor event in Beaverton, while Democrat John Kerry drew fifty thousand to a rally at *Waterfront Park*.

**Bill and Helen Gordon
& the Jewish Community Center**

In 1995, **Bill Gordon** (1908–) received the first Gladys
McCoy Volunteer Award from retired JUDGE MERCEDES DEIZ
E1 on behalf of Multnomah County. Bill and his wife,
Helen (1912–1984), arrived in Portland in 1953 to work
at the **Jewish Community Center** at *1636 SW 13th
Avenue*. That center, which was destroyed by "urban
renewal" in 1971, was renamed the Mittleman Jewish Community Center and moved to the Southwest
suburbs. In 1914, the center had been established because
"other clubs would not allow Jews to become members."[9] The Gordons were active in peace and civil rights
actions and later in the Gray Panthers, and Judge Deiz
especially remembered them for "all kinds of civil rights
activities for things Oregon so badly needed." A plaque
at PSU honors Helen with these words: "Because of her
love for children and her energy in their behalf, Oregon
is a richer community."

20 Fern Gage

In 1996, the children of **Fern Gage**, a Portland peace activist
since 1945, donated her library to the organization in which
she was most active, the FELLOWSHIP OF RECONCILIATION D9 at *6437
SW Virginia Avenue*. Gage, who began working in church
and civil rights groups, was also a supporter of the WOMEN'S
INTERNATIONAL LEAGUE FOR PEACE AND FREEDOM (WILPF) B18. Evelyn
Murray (1911–1996), another Portland WILPF member, was
especially active in the campaign against chemical warfare in
the 1970s.

21 Ace Hayes

Portland's leading muckraking journalist, **Ace Hayes**,
published his *Free Press* and held monthly "Secret
Government" seminars at The Clinton Street Theater
at *2522 SE Clinton Street* until his death in 1998. His
encyclopedic knowledge of government scandal and
cover-ups attracted some conspiracy theorists, but his

own 1993 investigation uncovered corrupt Portland Rᴇᴅ Sǫᴜᴀᴅ F26 activities, such as its link to the Anti-Defamation League of the Jewish community and the FBI.

 22 Portland Community College's "Remember"

A Northwest labor history mural, **"Remember,"** was dedicated at Portland Community College's Sylvania Campus in 1999. Sponsored by campus unions, designed by art faculty member Bill Garnett, and painted by his students, the mural depicts, among others, Dʀ. Mᴀʀɪᴇ Eǫᴜɪ B6, Jᴜʟɪᴀ Rᴜᴜᴛᴛɪʟᴀ F10, the early Wobbly martyrs, as well as today's Northwest Tree Planters and Farm Worker's United (PCUN), and Jobs with Justice.

 23 Woody Guthrie

Woody Guthrie D2, world-famous composer of our national folk anthem, "This Land is Your Land," is one of the few radicals officially honored in Portland. However, he is not honored by the City of Portland, but rather stealthily by the federal government's **Bonneville Power Administration (BPA)**. In 2001, with almost no publicity, the administration named the driveway at its headquarters "Woody Guthrie Circle" and erected three stones inscribed with verses from his songs "Roll on Columbia" and "Pastures of Plenty." A large tapestry of Guthrie also hangs in the lobby of the BPA building at 905 NE 11th Avenue. Much of the credit for the memorial goes to two BPA employees: folk singer Bill Murlin and retired employee Elmer Buehler, who drove Guthrie around the Columbia River region in 1941 and rescued some of his recordings that the government intended to discard.

In contrast, a year before the 2001 dedication, Guthrie's name was removed from the BPA's substation in Hood River when ownership was transferred to the Hood River Electric Co-op. Hood River's anti-Communist business leaders, who also removed Japanese American names from the town's honor roll during World War II, objected to the original designation in 1990. In 2000, they pressured the Co-op board to rename it for Willard Johnson, its first manager. They acted with unintentional irony, having forgotten that Johnson himself had strongly supported the Guthrie name against the local opposition, declaring that the "world would be better off with a few more Woody Guthries in it."

 Anarchist Convention 1993

"The Great Anarchist Riot" was the tongue-in-cheek label applied to the **1993 Anarchist Convention** outside the former X-Ray Café at **SW 3rd and Burnside Street**. Casualties included broken windows, bruises, and national media attention.

 The CIA & Scott D. Caplan

Scott D. Caplan, of the law firm of Jordan, Caplan, Paul, and Etter, fronted for a CIA cutout company, Bayard Foreign Marketing, LLC, which in 2004 was exposed as a key component of the Bush administration's "extraordinary rendition" program. Caplan's firm's offices in suite 755 of the Pittock Block, **921 SW Washington Street**, was also the Bayard address for the purpose of buying and owning the civilian jet the CIA used most often to kidnap suspected terrorists and take them to be tortured in cooperating countries or in the CIA's own secret prisons. Portland Peaceful Response held a protest at the offices in September 2005.

An earlier CIA contact in Portland (1949–1950), to whom prospective job seekers and information peddlers were referred, was a Mr. J. S. Bailey, with an office in room 414 of the Lewis Building downtown.

 The Portland Police Red Squad

The Red Squad of the Portland Police Bureau has been a notorious presence in Portland since before the World War I Red Scare. But because it still constitutes the city's political police as the Bureau's Criminal Intelligence Unit and operates from the tenth floor of police headquarters at **1111 SW 2nd Avenue**, its site is placed at the most contemporary chronological place in this guide—the end. In recent years, its surveillance and reporting have been focused on anarchist groups and antiwar, May Day, and environmental protests.

Until 2005, the city ordered two of its Red Squad members to join the FBI in Portland's Joint Anti-Terrorism Task Force (JTTF). That was the year the city council voted to make Portland the first city in the nation to condition continued assignment of its police officers on the FBI's granting of full oversight on their activities to the mayor and the chief of police. The FBI refused and the two officers were withdrawn. A Portland activist, Red Emma, wrote JTTF's secret theme song to the tune of "Every Breath You Take" by The Police. It begins:

> Every breath you take
> Every move you make
> Evidence we'll fake of the laws you break—
> We'll be watching you

Throughout its long history, the Red Squad has drawn most of its members from the ranks of ideologically extreme right-wing officers. In the 1930s, when the Red Squad had its office in room 428 of what is now the Oregon Pioneer Building at SW Stark Street and 3rd Avenue (then called the Railway Exchange Building), it functioned as an outspoken right-wing political gang funded with public and private funds. According to a scathing report by Gus Solomon and several other leading attorneys, the Red Squad spent its money on infiltrating and spying on labor and political organizations, organizing raids and provocations, and engaging in violent strike suppression. It even operated a clearinghouse for employers to blacklist leftists as potential employees. The Red Squad's leader was the right-wing ideologue, Walter B. Odale, a Portland police patrolman whose claimed rank of captain was actually in the U.S. Army Reserve. He supervised dangerous provocateurs like George Marion Stroup, who was never a sworn police officer but an American Legion anti-subversive activities agent, the violent provocateur Hal Marchant, and former bootlegger Merriel R. Bacon, who masqueraded as a Communist Party member.[10] During the McCarthy Era, the Red Squad was headed by another extremist, Detective William D. Browne, once the only member of the American Legion's "Americanization" Committee.

A warning to the Mayor from the head of the Red Squad:
CONFIDENTIAL
Portland, Jan. 6, 1949
To: Mayor [Dorothy] Lee
   Chief of Police
   F.B.I.
   File
A group of Communists and sympathizers are attempting to promote a movement among the colored people of the city to bring "Mass Pressure" to bear on the new Mayor's administration to force passage of what they call a Civil Rights Ordinance which would require hotels, restaurants and theaters and other places of business which serve the public to cater to colored people on the same basis as to whites and to make it unlawful for them to refuse to do so.
—W. B. Odale, Captain, Portland Police Bureau

Against all evidence, every mayor—from Joe Carson in the early 1930s to Vera Katz in 2004—has denied the Red Squad's existence; although sometimes they only stonewalled by saying that the police bureau's table of organization did not include a "Red Squad." Such false denials were frequently exposed when the Red Squad's routinely unlawful behavior was uncovered in the press or in other investigations. In 1996, a Multnomah County court found that undercover Red Squad spy Larry Siewert, who was assigned to track radicals and subversives, violated a Portlander's civil rights. Siewert actually spied and reported on the lawful activities of a wide range of peace, environment, and equal rights organizations. He later became Mayor Katz's personal bodyguard.

In 2002, the Red Squad was confronted with yet another scandal when the *Portland Tribune* revealed that Winfield Falk, a member of the extremist John Birch

Society and Red Squad member, had stolen Red Squad files from the early 1960s through the 1980s. The courts previously had ordered that the records be destroyed. Falk had hidden them on his property, intending to send them to his ideological comrades in private Red hunting groups in the east. After his death, the files were found and excerpts published in the *Portland Tribune*, which eventually deposited them in the Portland City Archives. Those files even included surveillance of future Mayor Vera Katz who, in her younger activist days, supported a farm workers grape boycott. Ironically, once in office, Katz became a devoted defender of the Red Squad against its critics until she left office in 2004.

1974 – Present Notes

1. "Ten years of Portland activism," *The Portland Alliance*, December, 1999.

2. *The Oregonian*, March 16, 2004.

3. For a historical account of the GLT identities movement, see *A Walking Tour of Downtown Portland: A Century of Gay, Lesbian, and Transgender Historical Sites* (1999), published by the Gay and Lesbian Archives of the Pacific Northwest and stored at the Oregon Historical Society.

4. David Kohl, "Portland's Centenary Wilbur Methodist Church: Probably the City's Most Significant Venue for Social Change in the 1960s–1970s." Unpublished Manuscript, 2005.

5. "Portland 1974–1999," *Willamette Week*, November 10, 1999.

6. *The Dispatcher*, October 5, 1979.

7. Sandy Polishuk, *Sticking to the Union: An Oral History of the Life and Times of Julia Ruuttila* (New York: Palgrave Macmillan, 2003).

8. Joan Kruckewitt, *The Death of Ben Linder: The Story of a North American in Sandinista Nicaragua* (New York: Seven Stories Press, 2000).

9. *Portland Tribune*, August 30, 2006.

10. Thomas S. Wilson, Ian Hart, Harlow F. Lenon, Chris Boesen, H. M. Esterly, and Gus Solomon, "Report of the Civil Liberties Committee" (National Lawyers Guild, Oregon Chapter, May 24, 1938).

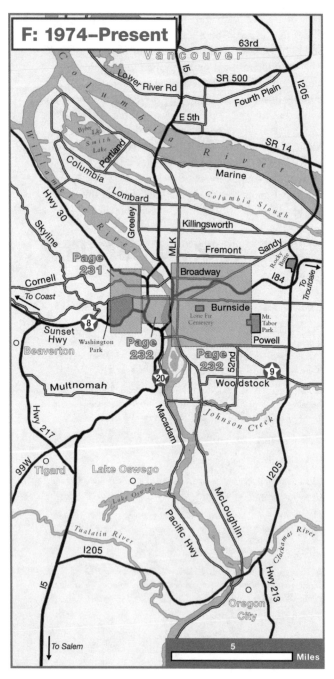

F: 1974–Present

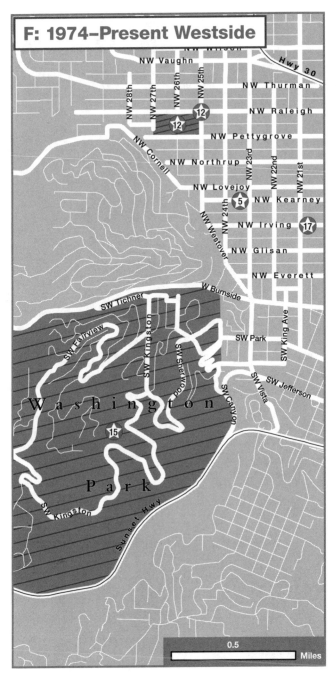

F: 1974–Present Westside

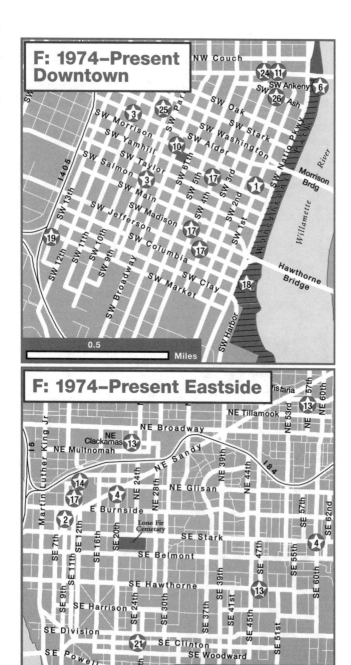

F: 1974–Present Downtown

NW Couch

SW Ankeny

SW Ash

SW Oak

SW Stark

SW Washington

SW Morrison

SW Yamhill

SW Alder

SW Taylor

SW Salmon

SW Main

SW Madison

SW Jefferson

SW Columbia

SW Clay

SW Market

SW Harbor

SW Park

SW 6th

SW 5th

SW 4th

SW 3rd

SW 2nd

SW 1st

SW Naito Pkwy

SW 13th

SW 12th

SW 11th

SW 10th

SW 9th

SW Broadway

I 405

Waterfront Park

Willamette River

Morrison Brdg

Hawthorne Bridge

0.5 Miles

F: 1974–Present Eastside

Tistaria

NE Tillamook

NE Broadway

NE Clackamas

NE Multnomah

NE Sandy

NE Glisan

NE Broadway

E Burnside

Lone Fir Cemetery

SE Stark

SE Belmont

SE Hawthorne

SE Harrison

SE Division

SE Powell

SE Clinton

SE Woodward

Martin Luther King Jr.

I 5

I 84

NE 53rd

NE 57th

NE 60th

NE 24th

NE 28th

NE 39th

NE 44th

SE 7th

SE 9th

SE 11th

SE 12th

SE 16th

SE 20th

SE 24th

SE 26th

SE 30th

SE 37th

SE 39th

SE 41st

SE 45th

SE 47th

SE 51st

SE 55th

SE 57th

SE 60th

SE 62nd

0.5 Miles

The Portland Labor College and Portland Labor Players II made a brief comeback in the late 1970s. They performed the play *Season of Silence*, depicting historic attacks on Chinese workers. *Norman Diamond*.

The Harbor Club was Portland's preeminent gay bar until city officials forced it to close in 1965. Its marquis can be seen on the far right side of this photo. *Oregon Historical Society, OrHi52847*.

 5 Bill Walton was the Portland Trail Blazers counter-culture center in the late 1970s. He was accused by the Red Squad F26 of joining anti-Vietnam protests and associating with radicals in Portland. *Oregon Historical Society, OrHi82630.*

 8 Stew Albert, longtime radical activist, moved to Portland in 1985. This photo shows him in Berkeley, California, at a rally in 1969. *Robert Altman.*

Francis J. Murnane led the ILWU and defended radicals his entire life. The wharf named after him is located on the west bank of the Willamette River, at the foot of SW Ankeny Street. *Colin Smith.*

Francis J. Murnane (center), head of the ILWU C9, and Rene Valentine (left), the Portland newspaper strike director, marched in the 1960 commemoration of Bloody Thursday C9. *Oregon Historical Society,* OrHi17650

 Julia Ruuttila was one of Portland's most prominent and involved radical activists. There were few labor or civil liberties struggles that she didn't participate in. She's shown here, being arrested in 1966. *Oregon Historical Society, OrHi23920.*

Martina Gangle Curl was photographed with the leader of the Red Squad F26, John Keegan, on July 15, 1941, in an attempt to paint her as a traitor to the labor movement. *City of Portland Archives, A2001-074.22.*

Martina Gangle Curl worked on a wooden sculpture. Her art can be seen around the city. *City of Portland Archives, A2001-074.56.*

 The first President Bush was surprised by the number of protestors—fifteen thousand—that marched up Broadway on January 12, 1991, against the invasion of Iraq. *Bette Lee.*

 President George H. W. Bush made Portland famous by declaring it "Little Beirut" in 1991. *Bette Lee.*

 In 1991, over fifteen thousand protesters filled Pioneer Courthouse Square in an antiwar rally. *Bette Lee.*

 The second President Bush avoided the Portland city center in 2004 and appeared instead at the University of Portland. The protesters followed him there. *Bette Lee.*

 The Sylvania campus of Portland Community College is home to this mural of Northwest Labor history. Designed by faculty member Bill Garnett and painted by his students, the mural shows familiar faces and places of the struggle. *Colin Smith.*

 Ace Hayes was Portland's leading muckraking journalist. He published *Free Press*, held monthly "Secret Government" meetings, and investigated the Red Squad F26 until his death in 1998. *City of Portland Archives, A2004-005.*

A TRIBUTE TO
woody guthrie

STOREFRONT THEATRE
933 N. RUSSELL
fri & sat. march 21, 22 – 8:30 pm
$2.50

Woody Guthrie D2 was quietly honored in 2001 by the Bonneville Power Administration when they named the driveway at its headquarters "Woody Guthrie Circle." This poster comes from a much louder tribute to Guthrie held at the Storefront Theater in 1975. *Barbara Davis.*

This photo demonstrates the extent to which the city was intent on keeping track of organized labor and Communist activity. The back of the photo reads: "Chief Niles—This photo was taken Wed, April 10, 1935. It shows the Communist gathering in the Plaza. I am keeping a photographic record of the 'Red' activities in Portland and will gladly supply the 'RED SQUAD' with copies on request. Paul Callicote." *Portland City Archives, A2001-074.80.*

Francis J. Murnane F6 led the annual Bloody Thursday C9 commemoration march for years as the head of the ILWU. This photo was taken of a July 5, 1967, march as the union moved east along SW 3rd Avenue. *Oregon Historical Society, OrHi101729.*

A Final Word

If you've come this far in *The Portland Red Guide*, it may be that you were interested, stimulated, amused, or maybe even angered enough by the alternate history it presents to see it through. If so, you are probably aware that it is hardly the last word on this large and controversial subject. Indeed, one reason it required more than a decade from inception to publication is that it never seemed—as indeed it still doesn't seem—to be done. New sites were constantly suggested to me by people, daily newspapers, and books. They all demanded investigation, so I was faced with a constant worry that someone or something important was going to be left out.

Finally a line had to be drawn and the fine and dedicated editorial collective of Ooligan Press drew it: Halloween 2006 became, for better or worse, the shut-off date because May Day 2007 had become the target publication date.

So apologies are due in advance for being unaware, for forgetting, or for overlooking both obvious and obscure sites that evoke Portland's radical past. Readers to whom those apologies are appropriate are invited to set the record straight by communicating with me via Ooligan Press—both to educate me and, possibly, to justify an expanded edition in the future. Especially invited are corrections of or additions to the listings and narratives.

But for now, please regard *The Portland Red Guide* in your hands as a modest start toward a more respectful public understanding and rehabilitation of a neglected part of Portland's common heritage.

Recommended Portland Histories

Readers of this guide will have no difficulty finding critical treatments of Portland's people and organizations in mainstream histories less receptive to radicals, Reds, suffragettes, civil rights militants, union organizers, and other dissenters. The books on this reading list offer fair portrayals of Portland's radical past.

Carl Abbott, *Portland: Gateway to the Northwest* (Northbridge, CA: American Historical Press, 1985).

Gordon DeMarco, *A Short History of Portland* (San Francisco: Lexikos, 1990).

Jewel Lansing, *Portland: People, Politics and Power, 1851–2001* (Corvallis, OR: Oregon State University Press, 2002).

E. Kimbark MacColl, *The Shaping of a City* (Portland, OR: Georgian Press, 1976).

E. Kimbark MacColl, *The Growth of a City* (Portland, OR: Georgian Press, 1979).

E. Kimbark MacColl (With Harry H. Stein), *Merchants, Money, and Power* (Portland, OR: Georgian Press, 1988).

Lewis L. McArthur, *Oregon Geographic Names* (4th ed.) (Portland, OR: Oregon Historical Society, 1974).

Elizabeth McLagan, *A Peculiar Paradise: A History of Blacks in Oregon, 1788–1940* (Portland, OR: Georgian Press, 1980).

Terence O'Donnell and Thomas Vaughan, *Portland: An Informal History and Guide* (Portland, OR: Western Imprints, 1984).

Eugene Snyder, *Portland Names and Neighborhoods* (Portland, OR: Binford and Mort Publishing, 1979).

John Trombold and Peter Donahue (Editors), *Reading Portland: The City in Prose* (Portland, OR: Oregon Historical Society, 2007).

Frequently Used Acronyms

American Civil Liberties Union   ACLU

American Federation of Labor   AFL

American Student Union   ASU

Black Panther Party   BPP

Communist Labor Party   CLP

Congress of Industrial Organizations   CIO

House Un-American Activities Committee   HUAC

Industrial Workers of the World   IWW

International Labor Defense   ILD

International Longshore and Warehouse Union   ILWU

International Longshoremen's Association   ILA

International Woodworkers of America   IWA

Joint Anti-Terrorism Task Force   JTTF

National Association for the Advancement of Colored People
NAACP

Northwest Liberation Front   NLF

Northwest Tree Planters and Farm Workers United   PCUN

Oregon Commonwealth Federation   OCF

Oregon Workers Alliance   OWA

Socialist Labor Party   SLP

Students for a Democratic Society   SDS

Subversive Activities Control Board   SACB

Women's International League for Peace and Freedom
WILPF

Works Progress Administration   WPA

About the Author

Michael Munk was born in Prague in 1934 and escaped the Nazi occupation of Czechoslovakia to Portland in 1939. He graduated from Hillside School, Lincoln High School, Reed College, and received an M.A. in Political Science from the University of Oregon. While a student, he worked as a causal longshoreman on the Portland docks, sold tickets at the Holladay Bowl's summer concerts, and drove a truck on wheat harvests in the Paulouse. His political activity began in the 1950s, when Mike became a local opponent of nuclear testing as well as a promoter of a Portland concert by Paul Robeson. As vice president of the Young Democrats of Oregon, he failed to win their endorsement of U.S. recognition of China, and was also unsuccessful in efforts to prevent the firing of a philosophy professor by Reed College. In 1959, he was ordered to leave Oregon by the federal government—whose domination of South Korea he witnessed as a drafted member of the U.S. Army.

After his military service, he was a national affairs editor of the leftist New York newsweekly, the *National Guardian* and, after receiving his PhD in Politics from New York University, taught political science for more than twenty-five years at the State University of New York at Stony Brook, Roosevelt University in Chicago and Rutgers University before retiring back to Portland.

Since his return, he has published on local radical history and culture in the *Oregon Historical Quarterly*, the *Pacific Northwest Quarterly*, and *Science & Society*. His column, "Our Radical Past" was a monthly feature in the *Portland Alliance* for several years. Prior to this Portland *Red Guide*, his most recent articles include "John Reed: Political Provocateur" in *Portland Monthly* (September 2006) and "McCarthyism Laid to Rest?" in *Reed Magazine* (Spring 2006).

Index

Ooligan Press

Ooligan Press takes its name from a Native American word for the common smelt or candlefish. Ooligan is a general trade press rooted in the rich literary life of Portland and the Department of English at Portland State University. Ooligan is staffed by students pursuing masters degrees in an apprenticeship program under the guidance of a core faculty of publishing professionals.

Special thanks to T. H. McKoy V, Jason L. Schmidt, and David Banis in the Portland State University Center for Spatial Analysis and Research for their help, guidance, and long hours spent mapping our city.

Thanks to Icky A, the Oregon Historical Society, Brian Johnson at the Stanley Parr Archives and Records Center, Bette Lee, Colin Smith, the ILWU, Reed College, Judy Albert, Larry Armstrong, Priscilla Carrasco, Hank Curl, Norm Diamond, Rick Rubin, Carl Saltveit, Brent Schauer, Dennis Stovall, and especially to Michael Munk for the images that tell this story.

EDITING Lead Editors: Terra Chapek and Gloria Harrison. Andrea Deeken, Haili Graff, Pamela Ivey, Miala Leong, Pat McDonald, Laura Meehan, Jon Sanetel, Joanna Schmidt, Irene Ridgway, and Erin Woodcock.
Indexing: Pamela Ivey.

DESIGN Lead Designers: Abbey Gaterud and Alan Dubinsky. Andrea Deeken, Angela Hodge, Jennifer Lawrence, Pat McDonald.

MARKETING Lead Publicist: Carson K. Smith.
Liz Fuller, Jay Evans, and Patrick Haas.